THE GREAT NO
RAILWAY IN TH
WEST RIDING

Part One - Doncaster - Wakefield - Leeds - Bradford
Dewsbury - Batley - Pudsey - Methley Joint

Martin Bairstow

Bradford Exchange on 1 September 1967. Low Moor based "Black Five" No 44694 has the up "Yorkshire Pullman" portion which it will take as far as Leeds City. Sister loco 45208 backs into platform 10 with the "Devonian" portion which will follow the Pullman to Leeds. Steam finished in the West Riding on 1 October, when both locos were withdrawn for scrap.   *(Roger Hepworth)*

Published by Martin Bairstow, 53 Kirklees Drive, Farsley, Leeds
Printed by The Amadeus Press, Cleckheaton, West Yorkshire

Introduction

The Great Northern Railway was incorporated in 1846 to provide a more direct route from London to Leeds and York than that which had been available since 1840 via Rugby and Derby.

By 1852, the Company had completed what we now know as the southern section of the East Coast Main Line between Kings Cross and Doncaster. Great Northern trains were obliged to continue their journeys to Leeds and York by running powers over rival lines because the company's own plans to reach these cities direct had, for the time being, been frustrated.

Once it had established its foothold in the West Riding, the Great Northern went on to build a local network much of which was heavily engineered, scenic, steeply graded, and a test for the locomotives and crews who had to work it.

Unfortunately, many of the West Riding towns reached by the Great Northern were also served by other railways which had arrived earlier, often by easier and therefore faster lower lying routes.

The Great Northern Railway disappeared as an independent company at the end of 1922 though the name tended to live on to describe that part of the LNER and British Railways. Even today, post privatisation, suburban services out of Kings Cross as far as Cambridge and Peterborough are marketed as Great Northern. The main line and London suburban routes thrive but nothing remains of the West Riding network except between Doncaster, Wakefield, Leeds and Bradford. Other towns continue to be rail served: Morley, Batley, Dewsbury, Castleford, Halifax, Keighley, Shipley. But in every case it was the Great Northern line which succumbed to rationalisation in 1950s and 60s leaving the tracks of its one time rivals to carry today's much enhanced frequency of passenger trains.

Much of the closed mileage has been lost with little trace. A few memorials remain such as Tingley Viaduct which carried the Batley to Beeston route over the now

Contents

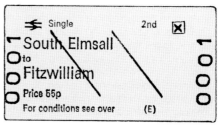

electrified Wakefield to Leeds line. One can now walk or cycle most of the way from Dewsbury to Ossett, including Earlesheaton Tunnel.

Otherwise we're dependent on those who kept a photographic record and those who shared their recollections and experiences. .

This book traces the origins and history of the Great Northern West Riding network as far north and west as Bradford. The lines to Halifax, Keighley and Shipley feature in Part Two – The Queensbury Lines.

I'm grateful to everyone who has helped.

When Fitzwilliam re-opened on 1 March 1982, South Elmsall was still issuing Edmondson card tickets. Our friend Geoffrey Lewthwaite was first in the queue.

The dramatic change of gradient at the Dewsbury end of Ossett Station. 61016 "Inyala" has a Saturday Cleethorpes - Bradford in summer 1964.

(Roger Hepworth)

Trainee Clerk
John Holroyd finds his first employment at Dewsbury Central

The search is on for my first job and British Railways have sent me a free rail ticket from Leeds to York and return. A bus ride from home in Gildersome takes me to City Station and the 09.15 'North Briton' arriving York 09.46. There are about twenty of us hopefully assembled at the Railway Institute for a brief introduction and an aptitude test in the main hall at 10.30. Happily this proved no great hardship and I left at 12.40 for a bite of lunch, a visit to the nearby Railway Museum properties and drifted home to await results.

A week later, Friday 16 September 1955, another free ticket takes me on the 12.42 train from Leeds to the York Railway Offices. Here I face an interview panel and medical examination and again head for home in anticipation. On Monday 19th a letter arrives saying I have been accepted as a Trainee Clerk and this is followed on Wednesday by a letter from Leeds Aire Street offices. I immediately don my coat and go to Leeds where I have another short interview and learn that my training will commence at Dewsbury Central Station on Monday 26 September. It just remained for me to collect an insurance card from Morley Youth Employment Office and cycle to Dewsbury to locate the Central Station for my first day at work.

The relief Station Master made me welcome at 09.00 on Monday and showed me round. His office was in the main platform buildings whereas my base was to be the Booking Office at ground level with only the overhead rumble of trains and the cries of the market traders for entertainment.

There was plenty of work to be done by the clerical staff, parcels traffic occupying a lot of our time, principally fibre boxes for the local dyers and cleaners' factories. Market traders parked their equipment trolleys under the arches for a weekly rental and Coal Waybilling for Hickleton Colliery was a daily chore.

I learned how to 'Take Off' a balance against ticket, parcel label and luggage-in-advance transactions. The first ticket I sold was a single to Lincoln at 9s. 11d. Fares were printed on the regular stock of tickets but less usual destinations had to be looked up in the fares manual and then uplifted to the present-day charge by reference to the current conversion booklet. If there was not a fare listed for any destination it was necessary to send a 'Faro' telegram to head office to request the base value which was then written in the manual.

The ticket racks had to be kept topped up from the main supply in drawers beneath the window. Consecutive numbering needed checking with each new batch and orders placed for more tickets as stocks dwindled. All our tickets were Edmundson cards which needed dating at the moment of sale – on both ends in the case of returns. Ordinary singles and returns were green, Day tickets blue, Excursions cream and Zones (Dog, Bicycle or Pram tickets) were red.

Monday evenings I attended 'Passenger Station Work and Accounts' classes at the Leeds Aire Street Offices between 18.30 and 19.30. Tuesday evenings likewise was 'Goods Station Work and Accounts.' I had a free pass for the train to Leeds valid on these days.

First week's pay amounted to £3 5s. 2d. Lunch at the nearby Playhouse Restaurant cost 3s. 1d. inclusive of coffee at this time.

There were four clerks involved in running the Office. Fred Ingham (to Cleckheaton) was replaced by Bill Donelly (from Headingley) as Chief Clerk on 17 October. The other three clerks, alternating early, middle and late turns, were Tom Howells of

The staircase leading up to the island platform at Dewsbury Central. *(John Holroyd)*

Thornhill, Bill Boden of Westerton and Jack Waterworth from Morley. I took on middle turn, 10.00-18.30, from Monday 19 December. Early turn ran from 6.30 to 13.00 (6.30 to 12.15 Saturdays). Late turn was 15.30-22.00 (Starting 14.00 Wednesdays). Porters were on duty earlier and later than the clerical staff so I never needed a key.

On Monday 28 November 1955 Station Master E.N. Pearson took over from the reliefs and he took me under his wing until I was transferred to Stanley in January 1956. Eric went on to Bridlington a couple of years later and stayed there until his retirement.

Occasional errands to check parcel deliveries with our associates at Wellington Road; The collecting of 6d. outstanding account from Newton Studios; Much laughter from Eric, the Undertakers' Suppliers lad; Upheaval during repainting; Two days when the Auditors dropped in . . . All served to relieve our otherwise daily routine. My cycle rides from Gildersome to start early turn on icy mornings were a good lesson in steering without wobbling. My last day at Dewsbury Central was Saturday 28 January 1956 when I did the coal waybills and filled in the weekly 'Pink Return.' This form compared the current weeks' figures with those of the same week last year, expecting an explanation of any major fluctuations.

I was instructed to report to Stanley Station on Monday 30 January as assistant to the regular clerk at this busy time in the Rhubarb Season. My father and I cycled to locate Stanley on the Sunday in readiness for my move. The round trip, with a variety of permutations, was about 18½ miles.

I arrived at the deserted station at 09.00 and porter 'Young' Bill emerged from the Lamp Room to welcome me and took me to the Station Master's House door. Albert Tate was in the middle of shaving but invited me in and his wife provided a mug of tea. I then had a conducted tour of the site which comprised a signal box working the level crossing at the east end of the platforms, a goods shed, sidings on both up and down sides and the smallest booking office imaginable! At least there was a good view of passing trains!

Methley South Station came under the care of Stanley's S.M. There was a signal box here and two lady porters dealt with all passenger and parcel traffic. Two or three times a week the Stanley clerk used a free pass to ride along to Methley to balance the books and this job was shown to me on my first afternoon. Regular clerk Brian Padgett and I boarded the push and pull train (Loco 69696) and dealt with Methley's finances returning on the same (Castleford-Leeds) train at 14.49.

As my attendance at Passenger and Goods evening classes continued I developed a routine of travelling to Stanley by public transport on Mondays and Tuesdays, cycling on the other days I worked. Usually I would walk to Morley Top for the 07.51 or 09.52 train to Wakefield (B1-hauled), continuing to Stanley by B&S bus (fare 4½d.). I only once took advantage of my cycle permit for the train from Morley Top. In the evening the 17.31 train took me to Leeds, my ticket being an original Methley Joint Privilege Single costing 5d. I travelled home from the Leeds evening class by Yorkshire Woollen District bus which picked up in Aire Street.

Soldiers on parade at Ardsley Station.

(Martin Bairstow Collection)

'Black Five' No 45140 calls at Morley Top with the up 'White Rose' (Bradford Exchange to Kings Cross) on 31 December 1960, the day the station closed. *(D. Holmes)*

In February the printed stock of Leeds Day Returns ran out and we had to hand write blank day returns until more arrived. Although Beeston station was closed by this date we still sold tickets to Holbeck for passengers alighting at Beeston when Leeds United had a home football match.

My pay for the first week of February was £3 15s. 2d. inclusive of an increase of two weeks. I assisted the S.M. in making out staff payslips and obtaining insurance stamps from nearby Lake Lock Post Office. In addition to the staff at Stanley and Methley South (Clerks, Porters, Night Shunter, Signalmen) we also paid the level crossing keeper at Patrick Green on the E&WYU line half a mile to the north.

We booked in boxes of rhubarb from about 15.30 to 18.30 when the engine came to collect our vans and take them to Ardsley. 'Old' Bill got his pipe going and we had a roaring fire in the goods office stove. About a dozen local growers would fill three or four vans most nights and usually one on Saturday mornings. Occasionally we would be given a few sticks to take home. I twice relieved at Ardsley during this period and was required to telephone the full list of assembled rhubarb van numbers to Leeds Control. At about 20.45 the vans from various local stations had been marshalled for Kings Cross and Covent Garden. A clerk plodding up the sidings with a hand-held paraffin lamp would be frowned upon nowadays!

Although there were some commuters who would have travelled earlier in the day, I never sold a passenger ticket at Ardsley on my middle turn. But I did receive an enquiry from a young lad who came to the window asking if I knew the number of the A3 which had just gone by.

Brian Padgett handed in his notice so I held the fort until clerk Laurie Palmer started on 26 March. That afternoon I took him on the push and pull to learn the Methley bookkeeping procedure. 4-4-2T

67438 was working the train. Station Master Tate had the Ladies Waiting Room converted into an office for his personal use, a new outer door giving access to the Ladies toilets. He 'threw away' the Ladies Waiting Room sign and I still have it as a tangible reminder of those days.

Wednesday 28 March was the morning of my exam in Goods Station Work and Accounts at Leeds College of Commerce. The Passenger Accounts exam was on Thursday 5 April. On Easter Monday 2 April I sold 71 tickets for the 12.06 Half-Day Excursion to Scarborough. Just 16 passengers booked for a similar train on Tuesday. The Methley ladies didn't sell any tickets on either day but still claimed their overtime to see the trains back in the evening!

My visits to Ardsley allowed me to copy out a list of all the month-end forms which had to be compiled and, with the assistance of S.M. Stebbings of Lofthouse we established an acceptable routine. A copy of this list served me well over the coming year when I moved to Morley Low as a fully fledged clerk.

Stanley station closed on 31 October 1964. Albert Tate had moved to Arbroath and we kept in touch for many years until both he and then his wife, Polly, died. The station house remained in a ruinous condition until finally demolished to make way for new housing: 'The Chase', Aberford Road.

Dewsbury Central's market facade remains to this day. The main arches with their iron gates, the booking office window and smaller washroom window are infilled with stone. The main A638 Inner Ring Road runs along the course of the track and platforms.

An account of John's days at Morley Low Station can be found in the second edition of 'The Leeds Huddersfield & Manchester Railway – The Standedge Line' published in 1990 in the same series.

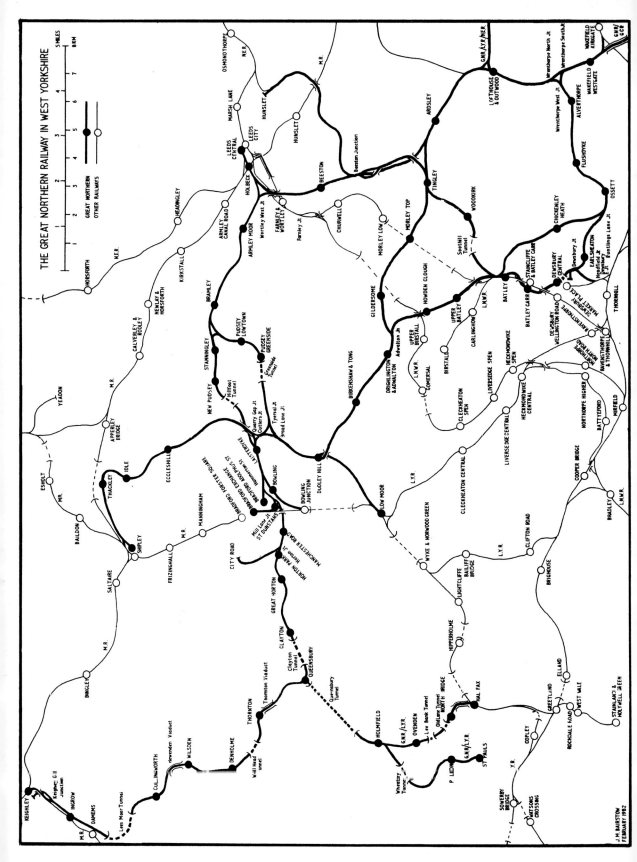

THE GREAT NORTHERN RAILWAY IN WEST YORKSHIRE

GREAT NORTHERN
OTHER RAILWAYS

J.M. BAIRSTOW
FEBRUARY 1982

Leeds Central

A4 No 60029 'Woodcock' prepares to leave Leeds Central with the 'White Rose' for Kings Cross on 16 March 1963.
(Martin Bairstow Collection)

For most of its 119 year existence, Central Station served primarily as the Great Northern terminus in Leeds. It catered also for the Lancashire & Yorkshire and Great Central Railways both of whose trains came into Leeds by running powers over the GNR.

Leeds Central was owned and had been built by four companies, two of whom abandoned it before it was even completed.

The first station in the centre of Leeds was at Wellington, opened by the Midland Railway on 30 June 1846. At that time, four other railways were in the course of promotion or actual construction. All four were heading towards Leeds where they desired to build a joint Central Station at a prestige site fronting onto Park Row.

The four companies were:

(1) The Great Northern Railway.
(2) The Leeds, Dewsbury & Manchester Railway, part of the Standedge Route, which was authorised in June 1845, incorporated into the London & North Western Railway in July 1847 and opened on 18 September 1848.
(3) The Manchester & Leeds Railway, which in 1847 changed its name to the Lancashire & Yorkshire Railway, had obtained powers in August 1846 for a line into Leeds from Bowling Junction, near Bradford. This line was eventually opened on 1 August 1854. It was used by the Lancashire & Yorkshire Railway but came into the ownership of the Great Northern.
(4) The Leeds & Thirsk Railway, which became part of the North Eastern in 1854. This was authorised in 1845 and completed on 9 July 1849.

These four embryonic companies deposited a Parliamentary Bill in November 1846 for their joint station on the north side of Wellington Street. The Leeds Central Station Act was passed on 22 July 1848 permitting the purchase of a significant area of land around what is today York Place, Park Place, King Street and Infirmary Street.

When the Dewsbury line opened on 18 September 1848. plans for the Central Station had not progressed at all so temporary facilities had to be provided on the south side of Wellington Street. These became the terminus both for the London & North Western Railway from Huddersfield and for the Lancashire & Yorkshire Railway whose trains from Manchester via the Calder Valley took advantage of this new route into Leeds via Mirfield and Dewsbury.

The same temporary station was also used by the Leeds & Thirsk Railway from 9 July 1849. Arriving trains used the Gelderd Curve to climb up from the Midland.

Last of the quartet of companies to run into the temporary Leeds Central Station was the Great Northern whose trains approached over the Midland Railway from Methley Junction, taking the south side of the triangle to avoid Leeds Wellington (the present goods line avoiding Leeds Station) then proceeded towards Armley before reversing direction and running up the Gelderd Curve to gain access to Central Station. This operation began on 1 October 1849, four weeks later than planned because of the 'Methley Incident.'

By the first half of 1850, with still no progress on the permanent Central Station, there were four companies using the temporary one. The Leeds & Thirsk was the first to express dissatisfaction by moving its business to the Midland Railway's Wellington Station from 1 May 1850. This simply involved their incoming trains staying on the Midland into Wellington instead of turning up the Gelderd Curve.

Five months later, the London & North Western Railway was able to effect a similar change with the opening of the curve between Copley and Whitehall Junctions. They also used Wellington from 1 October 1850.

The North Eastern (successor to the Leeds & Thirsk) and London & North Western continued to use Wellington until the opening of their own joint station at Leeds New on 1 April 1869.

Despite their pulling out of Leeds Central Station the North Eastern and London & North Western Railways remained joint owners of it. They both retained goods depots at or near to Leeds Central, the London & North Western on the high level adjacent to the passenger station on the north side, the North Eastern (originally Leeds & Thirsk) a little further north at a lower level with access from the Gelderd Curve.

The Great Northern also built a goods depot, between the Leeds & Thirsk and London & North Western establishments. It too was dissatisfied with passenger facilities at the incomplete Central Station. So on 14 May 1850 it withdrew from the joint ownership and transferred its passenger trains to its own temporary station built alongside its goods depot on the low level.

This meant that from 1 October 1850 the only company actually using the high level Central Station was the Lancashire & Yorkshire with its trains from Manchester arriving via Dewsbury.

Plans were dropped for the prestige Central Station, north of Wellington Street fronting on to Park Row. Instead a permanent structure was built on the site of the temporary one and completed by June 1852.

The Lancashire & Yorkshire Railway had hoped to build its own line direct to Leeds Central from Bowling Junction, near Bradford. It was unable to raise finance to achieve this. Instead the route was built by the independent Leeds, Bradford & Halifax Junction Railway. When this opened on 1 August 1854, it was worked by the Great Northern Railway. Like many small railway companies, the Leeds, Bradford & Halifax Junction preferred to remain as owners but not operators.

The new line approached Leeds alongside the London & North Western, crossing over the Midland at Holbeck then actually joining the LNWR at the entrance to the high level Leeds Central Station. Access to the low level GNR passenger station would have involved setting back down the Gelderd Curve then going forward again – an impractical proposition. So the GNR made peace with the three old Central Station partners, resumed its role as a quarter share owner and transferred all passenger traffic back to the high level station from 1 August 1854.

The Lancashire & Yorkshire Railway also remained at Central Station but from 1854 it approached by a different route. Trains from Manchester Victoria came via Halifax and Bowling Junction rather than via Dewsbury.

A1 4-6-2 No 60117 'Bois Roussel' pulling away from Leeds Central with 'The Queen of Scots Pullman'.
(Peter Sunderland)

The End of Leeds Central

Up until the mid 1950s, it had been considered impractical to concentrate all traffic on one station in Leeds. However, *Trains Illustrated* (May 1957) confirmed that British Railways were at last about to embark upon such a scheme. The August 1959 issue gave details of the plan which had been approved.

Central Station was to close and business was to be concentrated on Leeds City where passengers and parcels would be segregated. Passengers would use an enlarged facility at what was then known as City South – the former LNWR/NER New Station. City North, the old Wellington would be given over to handling parcels.

In order to get trains from the former Great Northern routes, from Doncaster and Bradford Exchange into Leeds City, a flyover was planned from near Holbeck High Level, crossing over the Midland thereby segregating passenger trains from the heavy flows of freight from the north via Skipton towards Normanton. A completion date of 1963/4 was hoped for.

Some work was carried out including the new canal bridge at the entrance to Leeds City reducing the number of tracks at this critical point from six to four. Also, an additional through platform was built on the outside of the train shed at City South. Then, in 1961, work was suspended.

Modern Railways (September 1963) announced a fresh go-ahead with a 1965 completion date. The scope of the work had been reduced chiefly by eliminating the flyover, forcing Great Northern traffic to descend a new Whitehall curve alongside Holbeck High Level. Trains from Doncaster were afforded a different route into Leeds by commandeering the former LNWR line over Farnley Viaduct and connecting it to the GN at the new Gelderd Road Junction. This was eventually found not to help and was abandoned with electrification.

The new arrangements finally came into effect on Monday 1 May 1967. Leeds Central had closed early on the evening of Saturday 29 April and there had been only limited services into and out of Leeds City on the Sunday.

The "New" Leeds City

The remodelled station was designed at a time when rail travel was in the doldrums. Most local trains were expected to be withdrawn and hourly Inter City trains had not yet been dreamt of. The 12 platforms could handle the 1967 level of business but not the increase in both trains and passengers over the following three decades. Passenger facilities included the subway steps which made access difficult to platforms 6 to 12 for anybody encumbered with luggage, small children or other impedimenta. Disabled passengers were dependent on staff escorting them via one of the goods lifts.

A further rebuilding was completed in 2002, bringing the number of platforms up to 17, all of which can be accessed by escalators and passenger operated lifts. Part of the expansion was over the former Wellington platforms which had become derelict after BR abandoned most of its parcels business in 1981. The number of tracks on the western approach was increased from four to six.

The last passenger train from Leeds Central, the 6.10pm dmu for Harrogate explodes detonators as it departs on Saturday 29 April 1967.   *(John Holroyd)*

The Leeds, Bradford & Halifax Junction Railway

B1 4-6-0 No 61129 passing Armley Moor with the 1.20pm (Sundays) Harrogate to Kings Cross, diverted via Bowling Junction because of engineering work on 31 December 1961.   *(D. Holmes)*

This was the project which enabled the Great Northern Railway to begin consolidating its foothold in the West Riding.

By an Act of 1846, the Manchester & Leeds Railway (soon to be renamed the Lancashire & Yorkshire) had been authorised to build a line from Sowerby Bridge through Low Moor, Laisterdyke and Stanningley to Leeds. There was to be a branch from Bowling into Bradford. In the event the route from Sowerby Bridge to Bradford was completed by 1 January 1852 but no progress was possible on the link between Bowling Junction and Leeds. The Lancashire & Yorkshire sought powers to abandon this and other West Riding projects for which it could not raise finance.

The failure of the L&Y to reach Leeds disappointed supporters who had assisted the company in gaining authorisation for the Bowling Junction to Leeds line. In November 1851 they deposited their own Bill for the nominally independent Leeds, Bradford & Halifax Junction Railway which effectively took over the L&Y powers between Bowling Junction and the entrance to Leeds Central. The project had the support of the Great Northern Railway which seized the opportunity to gain direct access into Bradford, thus projecting itself into territory which previously had looked as though it would fall to the L&Y.

The Leeds, Bradford & Halifax Junction Railway Act was passed on 30 June 1852. Running powers were granted over the London & North Western Railway from Holbeck into Leeds Central and over the L&Y from Bowling Junction to Halifax. In return, the L&Y was afforded running powers from Bowling Junction to Leeds Central.

A second Act of 4 August 1853 authorised a branch from Laisterdyke to Bradford Adolphus Street and confirmed arrangements by which the Leeds, Bradford & Halifax Junction would be worked by the Great Northern Railway.

The line opened to the public including the Bradford branch, on 1 August 1854. Ten trains per day (four on Sundays) were operated each way between Leeds Central and Bradford Adolphus Street. In addition, the Lancashire & Yorkshire Railway diverted its main line traffic from Manchester via the Calder Valley away from the Dewsbury route, which it had been using since 1848, running instead through Halifax, Bowling Junction and over the LB&HJ.

The route is heavily graded with a climb at 1 in 50 from Holbeck to Armley followed by 3½ miles at 1 in 100 to the summit at Laisterdyke. From there the 'main line' to Bowling Junction fell, initially at 1 in 100, whilst the branch into Bradford Adolphus Street fell at 1 in 44. The biggest engineering work,

Laisterdyke Station looking towards Bradford in 1870.
(Frank Kipling Collection)

The cutting had to be widened for the new station opened in 1892. Paget Foulds, Station Master, is nearest the camera.
(Frank Kipling Collection)

The Leeds, Bradford & Halifax Junction Railway (on right) ended at Bowling Junction, where it joined the L & Y route from Bradford to Halifax. A train of empty carriages is climbing the 1 in 50 from Bradford Exchange with a banking engine in the rear.

is the 450 yard Stanningley Tunnel sometimes called Hillfoot.

An insight into early operating procedure, or lack of them, is given in a report by the directors into a collision at Bradford Adolphus Street during the formal opening celebrations on 31 July 1854. An engine got out of control on the 1 in 44 gradient from Laisterdyke and damaged passenger coaches in the terminus.

The driver had not been over the line before and was totally unacquainted with the gradients. The whole proceeding is characterised by a general want of knowledge of the line and especially of the gradients, which in some parts require care and skilful management. Your committee are of the opinion that somewhat more caution might have been used by all concerned in the management of the Railway on the day of opening.

Despite opposition from the Lancashire & Yorkshire Railway, the Leeds, Bradford & Halifax Junction was absorbed into the Great Northern by an Act of 5 July 1865.

Adolphus Street was convenient neither for Bradford City Centre nor for the interchange with other railways. In 1864, the LB&HJ had obtained powers for the 3/4 mile link between Hammerton Street and Mill Lane Junction whence running powers were obtained over the L&Y into Exchange Station. This opened on 7 January 1867. From that date Adolphus Street was used only for goods although it seems from our later examination of the Shipley Ledger that it may have been used for overflow passenger traffic because of extreme congestion at Exchange Station.

This problem was finally resolved in 1888 when the new ten platform station was completed at Bradford Exchange. The approach from Mill Lane Junction was widened to accommodate separate pairs of tracks for the L&Y and GN Railways. Preparation for this involved the opening out of the 133 yard tunnel in 1884.

In 1910, there were typically two trains per hour between Leeds Central and Bradford Exchange but there was no regular pattern whatsoever. Some trains stopped only at Stanningley, some ran all stations via Pudsey but this was not a hard and fast rule. There were also some stopping trains via Stanningley. There were quite a number of trains covering only part of the route with some starting and terminating at Bramley or Stanningley.

'Black Five' 4-6-0 No 44693 is ready to leave Bradford Exchange in 1967 with 'The Yorkshire Pullman' which it will take as far as Leeds.   *(D.J. Mitchell)*

Stanningley looking towards Leeds. The two platforms were connected by a subway. The signal box at right angles to the track dated from at least 1872 but went out of use about 1905. It later served as an office and store for the Civil Engineer's Department until demolition in 1976. Beyond it is the bay platform used by Pudsey trains between 1878 and 1893.

Electric trams took short distance passengers away from the GN but slow speed and breaks of gauge prevented any greater threat. Bradford City Tramways No 160 pauses at Old Road, Farsley on its way to Stanningley about 1912. The 4ft gauge line opened in 1900 and closed in 1942. On 9 June 1909 a through service began between Bradford and Leeds with 12 vehicles from each fleet adapted to change onto standard gauge at Stanningley. The journey took 65 minutes. The technology was not used anywhere else and was allowed to die in March 1918.

Laisterdyke looking towards Bradford in early 1963. The canopies had gone since the photo on page 11.

(Roger Hepworth)

13 Lancashire & Yorkshire trains left Leeds Central via Stanningley and Bowling Junction. These varied in status from locals going no further than Sowerby Bridge to the 'Vestibule Luncheon Car Train' which left at 1.00pm for Liverpool Exchange. The 'Belfast Boat Train' departed at 8.05pm for Fleetwood. This, too, conveyed a restaurant car and, after calling at Holbeck, ran first stop Halifax which was reached in 28 minutes, faster than any of today's trains.

There was, by 1910, only one Great Northern train between Leeds Central and Halifax via Bowling Junction. It was the decline in the local GN service which had led to the closure of Bowling Station in 1895. L&Y expresses did not stop there.

If we go forward to June 1953, the timetable pattern is similar but with slightly fewer through trains and none of the short workings. Some of the intermediate stations had long intervals between trains. There was no local service at all on Sundays – just two through trains from Kings Cross to Bradford and five trains from Leeds Central on the former Lancashire & Yorkshire service but with no intermediate stops between Leeds and Low Moor.

This was the standard of service at a time when bus services were at their zenith and car ownership had recovered from the effects of wartime petrol shortages.

Change was at hand. From 14 June 1954, the route between Bradford Exchange, Leeds Central and Harrogate was the scene of the first full scale deployment of diesel multiple units on British Railways. The eight 'Derby Lightweight' twin car sets 79000-7 and 79500-7 were described in *Railways Around Harrogate Volume Three*. They offered a half hourly frequency between Bradford Exchange and Leeds Central going forward to Harrogate hourly. They also gave a stopping service between Bradford and Leeds via Pudsey almost at hourly intervals. They ran on Sundays – through to Knaresborough in Summer – but with no intermediate stops between Bradford and Leeds.

Steam trains continued from Leeds Central to Manchester and Liverpool until they, in turn, were replaced by class 110 diesel multiple units from 1 January 1962. Operating hourly from Harrogate, these trains were incorporated into the existing diesel service. They travelled via Bradford Exchange leaving only one early morning mail/passenger train using the direct Laisterdyke to Bowling Junction route. This finally closed to passenger traffic in 1969 and to goods in 1985 having latterly been reduced to a single line with no actual junction at Laisterdyke.

Stanier 2-6-4T No 42616 heads the 10.23 Bradford Exchange to Kings Cross through St. Dunstans in 1967. The Queensbury line curves in from the left. *(D.J. Mitchell)*

A three car 'Calder Valley' dmu passing Quarry Gap in March 1962. It has just gone under the Shipley branch and is approaching Laisterdyke. *(Peter Sunderland)*

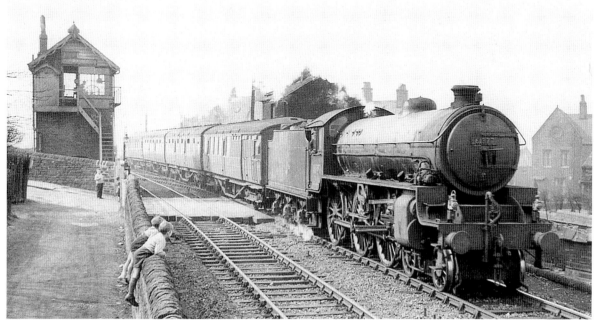

B1 4-6-0 No 61377 passing Hall Lane, between Bowling Junction and Laisterdyke with a Doncaster to Leeds Central local on 5 April 1959. It was diverted via Thornhill and Low Moor due to Bridge work at Wortley South. *(Peter Sunderland)*

Fairburn 2-6-4T No.42152 worked the last steam train out of Bradford Exchange, the 4.18pm to Leeds with through carriages to Kings Cross on Sunday 1 October 1967.

Back in 1967, there were generally two trains an hour between Bradford Exchange and Leeds comprising the loco hauled through carriages to London, the class 110 'Calder Valley' dmus from Manchester and assorted other dmus on Bradford-Leeds locals. In October 1968 cuts were imposed which left some gaps of an h our but these were gradually restored over the next few years. From May 1975, a 20 minute frequency was offered – one of the first fruits of the newly formed West Yorkshire PTE. From 1979, one train per hour started running through to York. In 1987 the basic service was stepped up to quarter hourly and from 1990 every train came through from Halifax or beyond.

New Pudsey

Just eight weeks prior to the closure of Leeds Central, on 6 March 1967, an additional station was opened called New Pudsey. Situated 3/4 mile west of Stanningley, it was described as the country's first Inter City park and ride station. It was one of only a tiny handful of stations opened on British Railways during the 1960s.

Contemporary thinking was that the future of passenger rail travel lay only in fast trains to London and precious little else. This begged the question how people were expected to gain access to this future rail network when, even then, road access to city centre stations was becoming increasingly difficult.

The answer was that they could park their cars at a new station situated adjacent to the Leeds Ring Road where they could join through trains to London. At first very few other trains stopped at New Pudsey. The first train in Bradford direction was not until 10.54am, Mondays to Fridays, even later on Saturdays. A few more stops were added from 1 May 1967 and again from September. Only from 1 January 1968 was there a comprehensive local service at New Pudsey following the closure of Stanningley.

There was no Sunday service until June 1981. Previous representations to BR had met with the response 'the station was built for businessmen and businessmen don't travel on Sundays'.

Gradually over the following decades, the original rather special concept of New Pudsey was forgotten. The through London trains were reduced in number then withdrawn altogether. The station assumed a similar function to any other commuter station with a car park. Incoming traffic began to develop with the building of nearby office blocks in the 1980s and the Owlcotes shopping centre in 1990.

155 345 calls at New Pudsey, bound for Leeds on 9 February 1991. There are now four trains an hour each way on weekdays and three on Sundays. A new ticket office and car park extension were commissioned in 2014. *(Martin Bairstow)*

N1 0-6-2T No 69483 at Leeds Central on 7 September 1953. *(G.M. Staddon/N.E. Stead Collection)*

79504/79004 on the 3.35pm Bradford Exchange to Leeds Central at Bramley on 14 June 1954, the first day
of regular diesel operation. *(D. Holmes)*

A 2 - 6 - 4T at the head of a Leeds - Liverpool express on the quadruple track section between Armley Moor and Bramley. *(M Goodall)*

The approach to Bramley Station, almost recognisable today except that the staggered Bradford platform is now accessed from the beyond the bridge.

A B1 takes the Pudsey line at Bramley with a modest payload.
(Mick York/ Richard Pulleyn collection)

Armley Moor looking towards Bramley. From the 1890s until 1968 there were four tracks between Wortley West and Bramley. The goods lines, on the left, did not have platforms at Armley Moor nor Bramley.
(Geoffrey Lewthwaite)

Fairburn 2-6-4T No 42107, of Low Moor Shed, powers up the 1 in 100 through Bramley en route for Liverpool Exchange via Bowling Junction and the Calder Valley route 1957. *(A.M. Ross)*

Stanningley for Farsley, looking towards Bradford. The mill, once rail served, stands on what is now the ASDA Supermarket!
(Geoffrey Lewthwaite)

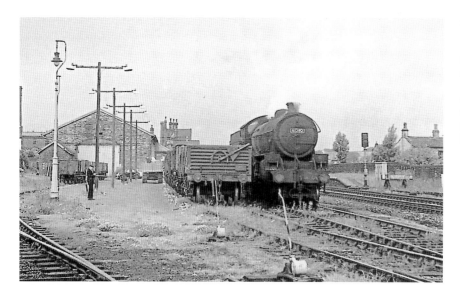

61030 "Nyala", minus nameplates and proper number plate, shunting at Stanningley shortly before withdrawal on 30 September 1967 when steam finished in the West Riding. Stanningley yard closed in 1979 but the goods shed survives as a builders' merchants.

"Deltic" No D9000 "Royal Scots Grey" approaching the site of New Pudsey Station with Pullman cars for Bradford Exchange on 16 October 1965. The area to the right is now the Owlcotes Centre.

(Martin Bairstow collection)

Duckett's Crossing looking towards New Pudsey in 1969. The automatic summersault signal dating from closure of the box in 1928 is being replaced by the four aspect colour light which is still there today.

(Richard Pulleyn collection)

Leeds – Bradford Electrification

The LNER planned electrification between Leeds Central and Bradford Exchange both via Stanningley and via Pudsey. Per a document dated August 1935, the lines to be electrified were the seven platforms at Leeds Central, four tracks through Holbeck, all four platform lines at Laisterdyke and platforms 6 to 10 at Bradford Exchange. Elsewhere, it was just the passenger lines and a few crossovers, a total of 29¾ track miles.

The LNER and its predecessor had been operating electric trains on Tyneside since 1904. The advantage over steam on an intensive suburban route was proven. But progress was stalled by the First World War and the difficult economic conditions which followed.

Eventually, with the aid of Government loans, they began work on the Woodhead Line between Manchester, Sheffield and Wath and on the commuter route from London to Shenfield. Both these schemes were delayed by the Second World War. The one they did manage to complete before 1939 was from Newcastle to South Shields.

Under the Standardisation of Electrification Order 1932, future electrification had to be overhead at 1,500v d.c. except for extensions to existing third rail systems. So South Shields was third rail but Leeds Bradford would have been overhead.

We're left to speculate whether d.c. electrification could have saved the Pudsey loop, whether it would eventually have been converted to a.c. and how a local Leeds Bradford electric would have fitted into the wider network.

In 1931, the Weir Committee had recommended electrification between London and Leeds. Had war not intervened, this might have happened a lot sooner than the eventual date of 1988.

Could it have been Pudsey? A class 506 EMU calls at Dinting with the 4.45pm Manchester Piccadilly to Hadfield via Glossop on 1 August 1963. The eight 3 car Glossop sets were ordered by the LNER in 1938 but delayed by war.

(Peter E Baughan)

Instead, in 1954 Leeds Central to Bradford Exchange became a pioneer DMU route. A twin powered Metro Cammell set leaves Pudsey Greenside for Bradford (despite the destination blind).

(Mick York/ Richard Pulleyn collection)

On 10 November 1964, 2 – 6 – 0 No 43072 lost control of an unfitted goods from Ardsley and crashed through the terminus at Bradford Adolphus Street. The crew jumped clear with minor injuries but the 14 year old loco was scrapped where it lay. Adolphus St finally closed to goods in 1972. Exchange Station closed on 14 January 1973 in favour of the smaller one just to the south, which is now called Interchange. The adjacent Victoria Hotel was built privately in 1867, bought by the GN in 1892, sold by BR in 1952 and is still open.
(Richard Pulleyn collection)

45208 heads the "Devonian" through the closed station at Armley Moor on 1 September 1967. 61030 "Nyala" works out its last days shunting the coal sidings which were to last until 1984. *(Roger Hepworth)*

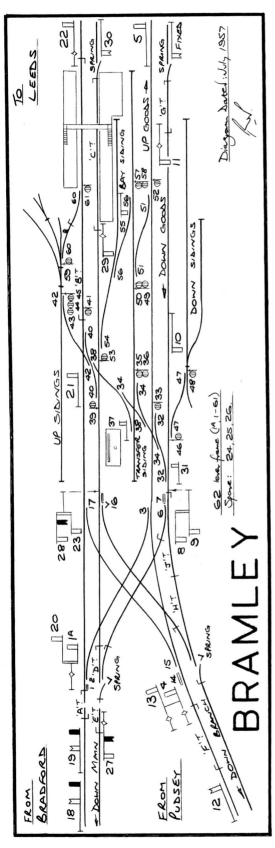

BRAMLEY

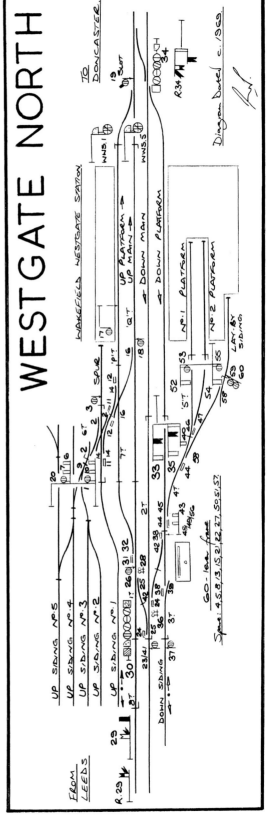

WESTGATE NORTH

Doncaster, Wakefield and Leeds

Class A3 4-6-2, No 60114 'W P Allen' recovering from a temporary speed restriction south of Sandal with the 'White Rose' from Leeds Central to Kings Cross in 1957.
(A.M. Ross)

The Great Northern Railway first reached Leeds Central from Doncaster on 1 October 1849 by running powers over the Lancashire & Yorkshire and Midland Railways via Askern and Methley Junction. The present day route via Wakefield Westgate came about later in two separate stages.

The Bradford, Wakefield & Leeds Railway

The title is confusing as this railway never served Bradford. It did, however, have its offices in Bradford. It was closely associated with the Leeds, Bradford & Halifax Junction Railway with which it connected by a triangular junction at Wortley, about a mile out of Leeds Central. It ran through Ardsley to Wakefield Westgate before curving to join the Lancashire & Yorkshire Railway at Ings Road Junction, just west of Wakefield Kirkgate.

The line opened on Saturday 3 October 1857. It was worked by the Great Northern Railway who, from 1 November, diverted their London trains this way to avoid both dependence on the Midland Railway and the reversal at Gelderd Junction outside Leeds Central. Great Northern traffic from Doncaster now travelled over the L&Y via Askern, Knottingley, Featherstone, Wakefield Kirkgate and Westgate.

The Bradford, Wakefield & Leeds Railway was responsible for building the line from Wakefield to Batley. It also promoted the Methley Joint (see later

chapter). In 1863 it changed its name to the West Yorkshire Railway.

In common with the Leeds, Bradford & Halifax Junction, the West Yorkshire enjoyed mixed relations with the Great Northern. On occasions both small companies threatened to break off the working arrangements with the GN and operate their own lines. To a partial extent they did but then had to hire rolling stock from the GN. For its part, the Great Northern threatened the West Yorkshire that it would go back to running via Methley Junction if condition of the track did not improve between Wakefield and Leeds.

Such problems were brought to an end in 1865 when the Great Northern took over the two small companies. They cannot have been all bad as they had both installed block signalling on all their lines prior to being absorbed.

The West Riding & Grimsby Joint

The Great Northern had failed in 1857, 1860 and 1861 to gain Parliamentary sanction for a direct Doncaster to Wakefield line.

On 7 August 1862, such powers were granted to the nominally independent West Riding & Grimsby Railway. The 'main line' was to run from Wakefield Westgate to Stainforth & Hatfield (between Doncaster and Scunthorpe) and so provide access

The main entrance to Doncaster Station leading direct onto the up platform. It was replaced by the present brick building in 1938, when the up platform became an island accessed by subway.

Photographed from the platform end at Holbeck High Level on 18 July 1953, A3 4-6-2 No 60062 'Minoru' has just left Leeds Central with an express for London Kings Cross. *(F.W. Smith)*

from the West Riding to Grimsby. A 'branch' was to run from Adwick Junction to Doncaster. The scheme had financial backing from the South Yorkshire and the Manchester, Sheffield & Lincolnshire Railways.

The Great Northern attempted to purchase the West Riding & Grimsby whilst under construction but would probably have been frustrated in Parliament by opposition from the Manchester, Sheffield & Lincolnshire which was in the process of taking over the South Yorkshire Railway. The solution was for the GN and MS&L jointly to purchase the West Riding & Grimsby which they did with effect from 1 February 1866, the day that the Wakefield to Doncaster section opened. Immediately the Great Northern diverted its London to Leeds traffic via the new line thus finally achieving its ambition of a direct route of 185¾ miles between the two cities, entirely under its own control. The Adwick Junction to Stainforth link opened in November 1866 permitting the MS&L to run a through service between Grimsby and Leeds. Part of the agreement for the joint line had included MS&L running powers from Wakefield Westgate into Leeds Central.

No 63633 joins the West Riding & Grimsby at Hare Park Junction in 1955 with a train off the link from Crofton Junction.   *(A.M. Ross)*

Class A3 4-6-2 No 60077 'The White Knight' passing Ardsley Engine Shed and South Box with an express from Kings Cross to Leeds in July 1961.   *(Peter Sunderland)*

The original Hemsworth Station was in typical West Riding & Grimsby style. View towards Doncaster.
(Alan Young collection)

It was replaced in 1912 by an island platform in the style of those on the Great Central London Extension. View also towards Doncaster. Rebuilding was made necessary by widening to four tracks. The up goods line, on the left, extended from Nostell to Hemsworth Junction where a lot of coal traffic diverged onto the Hull & Barnsley. The down goods on the right ran only from Hemsworth Junction to the north end of Hemsworth Station.
(Alan Young collection)

Nostell looking towards Wakefield.

Route mileage of the WR&G was brought up to 31½ by the opening of three short links in the twentieth century. The first was a 1½ mile single track branch from Castle Hills Junction to the new Brodsworth Main Colliery, which went on to become the largest in Yorkshire. This line opened for coal traffic on 18 May 1908. The Castle Hills south curve was opened by British Railways in 1969. The colliery closed in 1990, making the railway redundant.

The ½ mile double track curve between Carcroft and Skellow Junctions opened on 18 January 1909. It is used nowadays to stable and reverse the hourly DMU terminating at Adwick from Sheffield.

The link from Moorhouse Junction to Moorhouse & South Elmsall opened on 8 March 1909 giving access to Frickley Colliery. It closed about 1977.

In 1910, there were around a dozen local trains from Doncaster to Leeds plus a few intermediate stops by longer distance trains. The 1.30pm "Luncheon Car Express" from Kings Cross to Leeds and Bradford dropped a Huddersfield portion at Doncaster. This stopped at South Elmsall and Nostell before branching off at Hare Park to continue via Wakefield Kirkgate.

The Great Central offered two trains a day between Cleethorpes and Leeds which ran non-stop from Stainforth & Hatfield to Wakefield Westgate.

Besides the GN locals, there were a further six trains each way (two on Sundays) between Wakefield Westgate, Sandal and Hare Park, courtesy of the Great Central service to Barnsley Court House. Dating from 1882, this ran along the Great Central`s Barnsley Coal Railway which joined the West Riding & Grimsby by a double junction at Nostell. Sunday trains ceased during the First World War and the "Barnsley Bus" was withdrawn completely in September 1930. The route then survived for goods until July 1961.

In 1964, there were eight local trains a day between Leeds and Doncaster plus one to Cleethorpes and a semi fast which stopped at South Elmsall. Most served Ardsley until it closed at the same time as the Methley Joint at the end of October. Some trains went via Wakefield Kirkgate, rejoining the Doncaster line at Hare Park. There were no locals on a Sunday.

The service was reduced in November 1967 when Fitzwilliam, Hemsworth and Carcroft & Adwick le Street closed. South Elmsall remained open with around six trains each way. The stops at Wakefield Kirkgate ceased.

Fitzwilliam reopened in 1982, the first of a number of unstaffed wooden halts financed by the West Yorkshire PTE. Sandal followed in 1987 and Outwood the following year. In South Yorkshire, where grants were easier to obtain, more substantial structures appeared at Bentley in 1992 and Adwick in 1993.

The local service became hourly in 1987, worked by class 142 and 144 diesel units until 1989 when some class 307 electrics were brought from the London, Tilbury & Southend line. These were replaced in 1990 by three new four car units of class 321. In addition, since 1993 there has been an hourly diesel from Adwick to Doncaster which continues to Sheffield via Mexborough.

The full "High Speed" timetable was introduced in May 1979. Until then, the fastest times to London were achieved by only a few trains with limited load and limited stops. Marketed as "InterCity 125", the new trains had a streamlined class 43 loco at each end. The revolutionary feature was the consistent speed of trains spaced at regular intervals throughout the day, completing the 185¾ mile journey in under 2½ hours with as many as six stops.

Electrification was authorised in 1984 and completed in August 1988. Since then, most London trains have been push-pull formations with a class 91 at the Leeds end. But there are still some diesels, partly to cover diagrams which extend to non-electrified destinations and partly because there are only 31 electrics which is insufficient. The service has been half hourly since 2007 with almost all trains calling at Wakefield Westgate and Doncaster.

The Swinton & Knottingley

The Swinton & Knottingley, joint Midland & North Eastern, opened in 1879. It made south to west and east to north connections with the West Riding & Grimsby. The former, from Moorthorpe to South Kirkby Junction, is used today by expresses and locals between Sheffield and Leeds.

The Great Northern had objected to the Swinton & Knottingley in Parliament and had been bought off with running powers. The 1887 timetable shows four trains a day from Doncaster to Pontefract Baghill via South Elmsall. By 1910 the number was down to two and the service finished as a "temporary" wartime economy on the last day of 1916. The 1¼ mile link between South Elmsall and Moorthorpe North Junctions closed completely in 1928.

The diagonally opposite curve from Moorthorpe Station to South Kirkby Junction is still in business. From May 1967, the closure of Leeds Central brought a re-routing of most Leeds – Sheffield expresses away from the former Midland Main Line which had missed Wakefield. Instead they called at Westgate before continuing along the Doncaster line as far as South Kirkby Junction.

In 1973, they were diverted back onto the Midland because of mining subsidence between South Kirkby and Sheffield. Those which still served Wakefield Westgate were subjected to an arduously slow journey via Kirkgate to reach the Midland at Oakenshaw South Junction. What was needed was to reinstate the curve between Sandal and West Riding Junction which had been removed in 1938. Before this could be seriously considered, the subsidence problem moved and, from 1984, traffic was again routed via South Kirkby. The Midland Main Line was subsequently closed between Normanton and Swinton. Since May 1988, there has been a local service from Leeds to Sheffield, giving a second hourly stopping train between Leeds and Fitzwilliam.

The signalman and train recorder inside Westgate South box in 1959. The former is Jack Bancroft who later worked in Leeds Telegraph Office because he was a good operator of the single needle telegraph. *(A M Ross)*

Viewed from the box, J39 No 63612 approaches with a coal train from Barnsley via Nostell.

(A.M. Ross)

A Doncaster to Leeds local doing good business at Carcroft & Adwick le Street. The main building survives as a private house. The present station would be behind the camera.

The wooden structure at Hampole opened on New Year`s Day 1885. Doncaster is to the right. The Leeds bound platform is hidden in the cutting. Most local trains stopped but there was no Sunday service.

Hare Park & Crofton looking towards Leeds. The right hand route is the link to the L&Y at Crofton Junction which gave access to Wakefield Kirkgate under the 1882 Agreement.

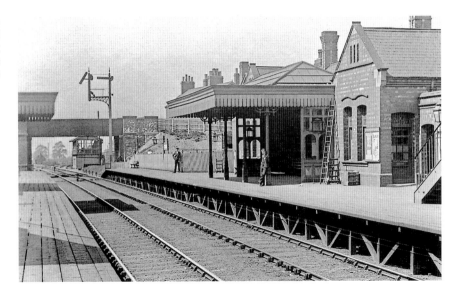

Fitzwilliam was an island platform opened by the LNER in June 1937. It was served by around eight trains each way but with nothing on Sundays. It closed in November 1967.

(Alan Young collection)

A replacement station opened in 1982, fractionally to the south. The up and down lines are separating to enclose the previous island platform which was accessed from the road bridge. The second span was required when the up goods line was commissioned in 1912. There was no fourth track as the down goods didn't extend this far. *(Alan Young)*

The West Riding & Grimsby Joint building survived at South Elmsall until the early 1980s but then the station became unstaffed and the building was demolished.

(Martin Bairstow)

Sandal looking towards Leeds. Closed in November 1957, it reopened 30 years later on the same site but with the longer name Sandal & Agbrigg.

Shortly after Nationalisation, BR held the Locomotive Exchanges, officially as a motive power experiment but perhaps also as a publicity exercise. 6018 "King Henry VI" of the Great Western and 35019 "French Line CGT" of the Southern Railway are seen at Holbeck with expresses from Kings Cross to Leeds on 12 and 17 May 1948. The Merchant Navy has an LMS tender for the water troughs, of which there weren`t any on the Southern.

(J W Hague, courtesy David Beeken)

2-2-2 No 879 stands in Wakefield Westgate at the head of an express from Leeds Central to Kings Cross. Built at Doncaster in 1894, the Stirling 'Singles' were designed for express work on lightly graded lines.
(Martin Bairstow Collection)

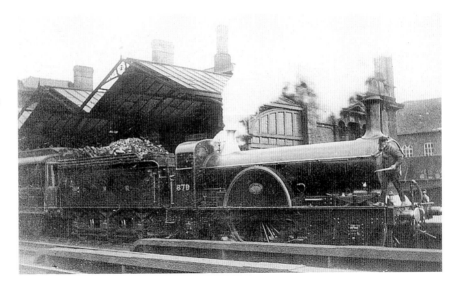

60029 'Woodcock' passing the closed (but still occasionally used) station at Beeston with a Leeds Central to Doncaster local on 17 June 1961.
(Martin Bairstow Collection)

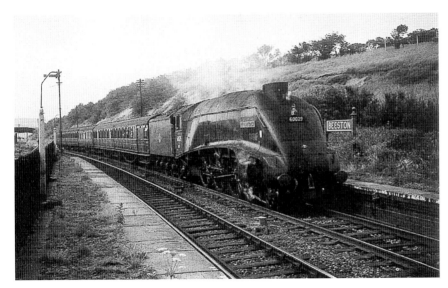

C14 4-4-2T No 67438 passing Beeston Junction with a local from Leeds Central.
The junction signal is for the Batley branch. The line curving to the right behind the train is the Hunslet goods branch opened by the Great Northern on 3 July 1899.
(A.M. Ross)

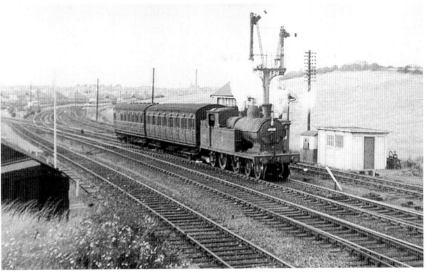

307122 calls at South Elmsall with a Doncaster to Leeds local on 22 December 1990.
(Martin Bairstow)

144 008 calls at Bentley with an Adwick to Sheffield service on 21 February 2015. In 1922, the Doncaster Regional Planning Report recommended that the Great Northern should provide a station at Bentley. The idea evidently found favour and the station opened in 1993.
(Martin Bairstow)

142086 calls at the then recently opened Sandal & Agbrigg with a Doncaster to Leeds local on 24 December 1987. *(Martin Bairstow)*

A class 110 "Calder Valley" set leads a six car formation working a local from Leeds Central to Doncaster over the junction at Hare Park on 6 July 1965   *(M Mitchell)*

When coal was still king, 40038 passes a slag heap between Carcroft and Hampole with a northbound mixed freight on 27 December 1973.   *(M. Mitchell)*

Between Bradford and Wakefield

Under a lowering sky, 45338 and 42084 climb away from Dewsbury towards Wakefield with the 8.52 (SO) Bradford to Cleethorpes on 11 August 1962. *(M. Mitchell)*

A reasonably direct route via Wortley was available between Wakefield and Bradford from the opening of the BW&L on 3 October 1857. Just one week later, a shorter but even steeper route was completed via Morley. Over the next 23 years, the Great Northern completed two more variants of the Wakefield to Bradford route, first via Ossett and Batley then via Dewsbury. The Lancashire & Yorkshire Railway also opened a direct Wakefield to Bradford route in 1869 when it completed the short link between Thornhill and Heckmondwike.

In more recent times all five of the routes just mentioned have been abandoned. Wakefield and Bradford are still connected by a rail but only via Leeds albeit that trains on both segments of the journey now run at an unprecedented frequency.

It was the coalfield and heavy industry that drew the railway into the area between Wakefield and Bradford. A branch from Laisterdyke to Gildersome was authorised by the Leeds, Bradford & Halifax Junction Act of 4 August 1853. Double track from its opening on 19 August 1856, the five mile line was steeply graded with short tunnels at Birkenshaw (106 yards) and Gildersome (156 yards). Heaviest traffic was coal from Adwalton field to supply Bradford.

Powers for the extension to Ardsley were granted to the LB&HJ on 10 July 1854, the same day that the

BW&L Act was passed. The 4½ mile section, also double track was opened on 10 October 1857. There was an intermediate station at Morley, latterly known as Morley Top which was almost directly above the LNWR tunnel and far more convenient for the town than the LNWR station at Morley Low. Tingley station first appeared in *Bradshaw* for May 1859.

Through carriages between Kings Cross and Bradford began to be worked via Gildersome from 1 December 1857.

A branch to Ossett was authorised by the BW&L Act of 23 July 1860. A single line opened for coal traffic as far as Roundwood Colliery on 6 January 1862. On 7 April the line reached Flushdyke which was known as Ossett for the next two years whilst it remained the terminus. Ossett itself opened on 7 April 1864.

In 1861 both the LB&HJ and the BW&L obtained Acts allowing them to extend and meet one another at Batley. The LB&HJ opened from Adwalton Junction to Upper Batley on 19 August 1863 reaching Batley itself on 1 November 1864. The station at Upper Batley was only a temporary structure. It was moved to Howden Clough in 1866, allowing a station to open there on 1 November following completion of the permanent facilities at Upper Batley.

2-6-4T No 42639 pilots B1 No 61013 on the 8.52 (SO) Bradford to Cleethorpes seen rounding the curve between Laisterdyke and Cutlers Junction on 1 August 1964. *(M. Mitchell)*

Fowler 2-6-4T No 42411 passing Dudley Hill with the Bradford portion of a train from Kings Cross about 1964. *(H. Malham)*

A Metro Cammell unit taking the Batley line at Cutlers Junction.

(Mick York/ Richard Pulleyn collection)

Ivatt 2 – 6 – 0 No 43079 passing Dudley Hill with a local freight towards Wakefield.

(Mick York/ Richard Pulleyn collection))

A Fowler tank heads the 1.23pm, Bradford to Kings Cross between Dudley Hill and Birkenshaw on 10 August 1960. To the left are the earthworks of the curve which was never laid to join the Low Moor line.

(M. Mitchell)

The BW&L reached Batley from the other direction on 15 December 1864. The track was single. There were seven overbridges, nine underbridges and short tunnels at Chickenley Heath (47 yards) and Shaw Cross (209 yards). There was no intermediate station until Chickenley Heath opened on 2 July 1877.

The Dewsbury Loop

So far, the Wakefield-Batley-Bradford line had missed Dewsbury. Powers for a branch were granted to the Great Northern Railway in July 1871. It was to leave the existing Wakefield to Batley line at Runtlings Lane Junction. It included a 179 yard tunnel at Earlsheaton, four overbridges and three underbridges. The steepest gradient was 1 in 53. It opened to goods on 1 May 1874 and to passengers on 9 September with a service of 14 trains each way (five on Sundays) between Wakefield Westgate and Dewsbury.

On 1 May 1876 a north to west curve was opened at Wrenthorpe permitting a through service from Leeds Central to Dewsbury of six trains weekdays and three Sundays. The track from Wrenthorpe to Runtlings Lane Junction had been doubled by August 1873. The line in to Dewsbury was double from its opening.

Powers to extend to Batley were allowed to lapse but were then revived in 1877. The link was finally opened on 12 April 1880. From the previous temporary Dewsbury station, it passed through a 213-yard tunnel to reach a new island platform station at Dewsbury Central. Between there and Batley it crossed twice under the LNWR mainline. In all there were six overbridges and five under. The steepest gradient was 1 in 53. At Batley, an island platform was provided on the east side of the LNWR station. Most through traffic was diverted off the Chickenley Heath line onto the Dewsbury route.

Passenger trains were withdrawn completely from the Chickenley Heath line in July 1909 having latterly been worked by a railmotor four times per day each way. The previous November, the Dewsbury & Ossett Tramway had opened with a frequent service passing Chickenley Heath Station. The Great Northern Railway had objected, unsuccessfully, to the Tramway Order on the grounds of the adequacy of their own service, the weakness of the road overbridge at Chickenley Heath upon which the tramway would be laid and the possibility that the electric current might interfere with the Railway's signalling and telegraph systems.

Bradford to Wakefield in 1910

The service begins with the 5.02am all stations from Laisterdyke to Wakefield Kirkgate via Ardsley. There is a 5.37am all stations from Batley to Wakefield Westgate which has come from Leeds Central via Beeston. The first departure from Bradford

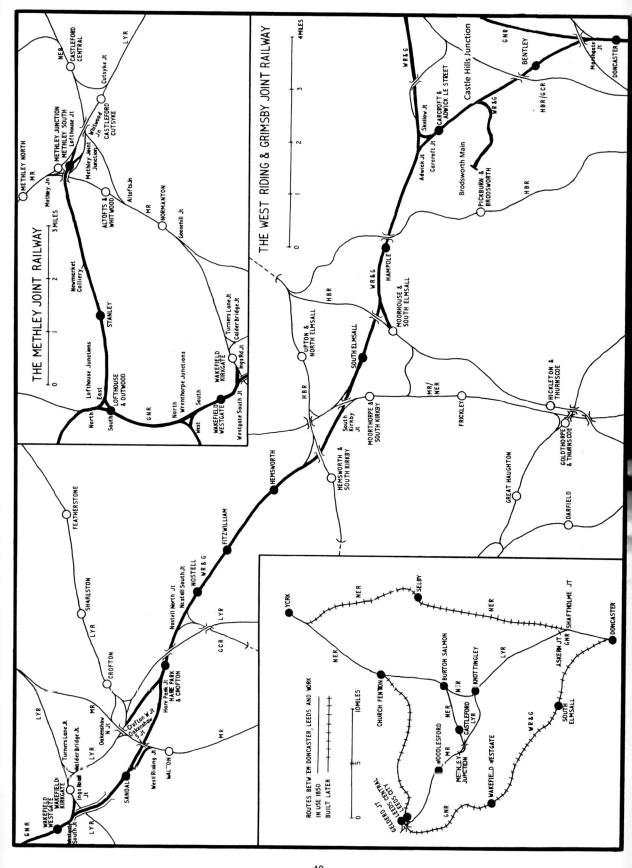

THE METHLEY JOINT RAILWAY

THE WEST RIDING & GRIMSBY JOINT RAILWAY

Castle Hills Junction

ROUTES BETWEEN DONCASTER, LEEDS AND YORK

IN USE 1850
BUILT LATER

40

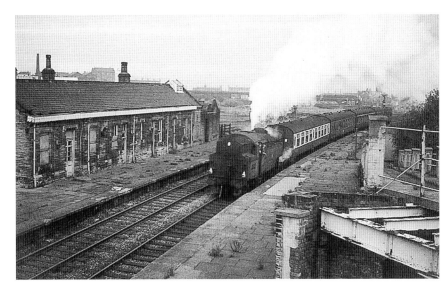

Dudley Hill saw occasional use by excursions after closure in 1952 but was rather derelict by 1966 when this 2-6-4T passed through with the Bradford portion of a train for Kings Cross. *(D.J. Mitchell)*

From 4 July 1966, remaining Bradford to Wakefield trains were re-routed via Wortley, leaving the Morley line virtually without traffic. But on Sundays in October, the Bradford to London portions were diverted back due to work on the new road bridge at New Pudsey. A Fairburn tank is brought to a stand at Birkenshaw on 30 October for the signalman to pass on some verbal instruction. The next day the through route was broken with complete closure between Birkenshaw and Gildersome.

(D J Mitchell)

B1 4-6-0 No 61033 'Dibatag' on a Bradford to Wakefield service at Drighlington in May 1952. *(B.G. Tweed/N.E. Stead Collection)*

Exchange is the 5.37am all stations to Wakefield Kirkgate via Dewsbury. This gives a connection at Drighlington into a 6.13 all stations to Ardsley.

The pattern is repeated throughout the day right up to the 11.18pm Bradford Exchange to Wakefield Kirkgate via Dewsbury. There is no regularity to the service but most stations are served at least once an hour. There are quite a number of trains starting from Drighlington, generally giving a connection for Ardsley out of a Bradford-Dewsbury-Wakefield train or vice versa. In some instances, both trains continue to Wakefield.

There is a Mondays only 6.07am from Bradford Exchange to Kings Cross which joins the Leeds portion, also Mondays only, at Wakefield Westgate and then appears to be joined onto a Nottingham-London train at Grantham. It gives an arrival in Kings Cross at 10.40, some 50 minutes before the daily first through train from Bradford.

The 6.07 stops at St Dunstans, Laisterdyke and Ardsley. It also has conditional stops at Dudley Hill and Gildersome 'to take up for London' and at Birkenshaw and Morley 'to take up for Doncaster and south thereof'.

The 7.25am Bradford Exchange to Kings Cross stops at St Dunstans, Batley, Dewsbury Central and Ossett. It also stops conditionally at Laisterdayke, Birkenshaw, Upper Batley and Earlsheaton 'to take up for London'. At Wakefield Westgate it joined the 'Breakfast Car Express' which left Leeds Central at 7.50am. There were similar London through carriages during the rest of the day.

On Sundays the service was more restricted with just eight trains from Bradford to Wakefield, most frequent in the evening. Five went via Dewsbury and three via Ardsley.

Looking north at Ardsley in August 1960. A coal train waits to come off the Gildersome line. The M62 now crosses at this point. *(M. Mitchell)*

Shaw Cross Tunnel on the Chickenley Heath branch in 1951. The track looks a bit rough. *(D. Ibbotson)*

J50 No 68935 heads past the closed station at Gildersome on 16 July 1963. *(M. Mitchell)*

J39 0-6-0 No 64760 passing Tingley with an afternoon freight in the Ardsley direction on 10 August 1962.
(M. Mitchell)

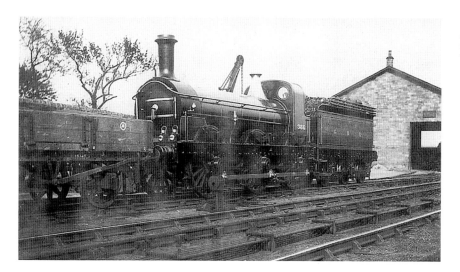

Great Northern 0-6-0 No 386 shunting at Morley Top. The engine was built in 1855 and withdrawn in 1902.
(D.J. Mitchell Collection)

J50 0-6-0T No 68915 climbing the 1 in 73/109 through Tingley with a transfer freight from Ardsley towards Morley Top in 1957. *(A.M. Ross)*

Tingley booking office in 1961, after closure.
(Peter E. Baughan)

Station closures

Many stations lost their Sunday trains permanently during the First World War. The 1923 timetable shows St Dunstan`s, Dudley Hill, Birkenshaw, Gildersome, Tingley, Howden Clough, Upper Batley, Batley Carr, Earlesheaton, Flushdyke and Alverthorpe without any Sunday service.

In those days, the stations were staffed whenever trains called. With fewer people travelling than on weekdays, but with overtime wages, the simplest thing was to keep all but the most important stations locked out of use. Morley fell victim during the Second World War. Drighlington followed soon after and by 1951, there were no intermediate stops at all between Bradford and Wakefield, just a handful of non-stop London portions.

Stations could still be opened specially for Sunday excursions. As an example, on 14 June 1959 there was a "Scenic Excursion by Tourist Train" to the Yorkshire Coast. Starting from Laisterdyke at 9.30 am, it picked up at Batley, Dewsbury Central, Ossett, Wakefield Westgate and Kirkgate, Normanton and Castleford. Patrons enjoyed 2½ hours in Whitby and four in Scarborough. Arrival back in Laisterdyke was at 12.05, just after midnight.

During the 1950s and early 60s, individual stations

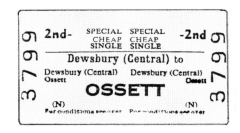

were closed on a piecemeal and seemingly haphazard basis. Between Bradford and Wakefield via Ardsley, there were ten intermediate stations. These closed on ten different dates starting with Dudley Hill in 1952 and finishing with Laisterdyke in 1966.

Between Drighlington and Wakefield via Dewsbury, there were nine intermediate stations. Flushdyke had closed in 1941 whilst Batley is still open. The other seven closed on six different dates, none of them duplicating the ten in the previous paragraph. Batley Carr was first to go in 1950. Dewsbury Central and Ossett were the last on 5 September 1964. Some of the earlier victims had continued to open occasionally for seaside excursions until that class of traffic became a victim of the Beeching Report.

Tom Chapman, born about 1903, was a signalman at Howden Clough in the early 1930s. He bequeathed a photograph album which has been made available by his widow, Mrs Annie Chapman via her nephew Ian Stringer. Unfortunately, the album contains only small format prints, many of them faded. The negatives were lost in the depth of time. None the less, the reproductions on this and the next page reveal something of contemporary life at Howden Clough.

Two photographs taken at the start of a blizzard in February 1933. (Above) looking up the line towards Drighlington. (Right) view from the signal box across the Main line into the goods yard.

(Tom Chapman)

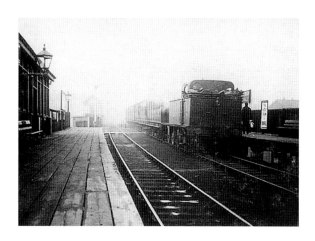

Anti clockwise from top left: An Ivatt 4-4-2T arrives at Howden Clough for Birstall with a Bradford to Wakefield stopping train in 1932: 4-4-2T No 4017 has temporarily abandoned its train opposite the signal box in order to detach cattle wagons: The enterprising staff have designed their own excursion publicity for the 1931 season: Self portrait at the lever frame in Howden Clough box. *(Tom Chapman)*

Complete closure between Adwalton Junction and Wakefield followed in February 1965 except that access remained from Wrenthorpe South Junction to Roundwood Colliery, east of Flushdyke, until October 1965. Bradford portions of London trains continued to reach Wakefield via Morley until July 1966 when they were diverted via Wortley. The through route was broken at the end of October 1966 between Birkenshaw and Gildersome. The remaining sections then closed as their remnants of freight business dried up. Last to go was an occasional wagon of steel over a single line between Laisterdyke and Dudley Hill which expired in 1981.

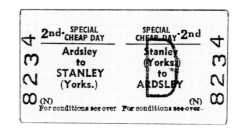

Dewsbury Junction seen from a double headed Cleethorpes to Bradford train on a Saturday in June 1963. The signal box opened in 1886 to control the two junctions; from Headfield and to the GN goods yard. More than half the 50 levers were spare after 1933 when the line from Headfield Junction closed. A new 20 lever frame was eventually substituted in 1955. The box closed along with the route from Adwalton Junction to Roundwood Colliery in February 1965.

(Roger Hepworth)

Viewed from a Bradford to Wakefield DMU, the GN goods depot at Dewsbury Railway Street. The line from Headfield Junction reopened on 15 February 1965 to preserve access to this yard on closure of the GN route through Dewsbury. This left what was effectively a branch from Dewsbury East Junction on the L&Y Calder Valley Line main line. It closed in 1989. Railway Street yard is now a retail park. *(Roger Hepworth)*

Seen from the derelict signal box, 61353 climbs through Howden Clough with the 12.00 Saturdays only Lowestoft to Bradford on 29 August 1964.   *(M. Mitchell)*

The 10.20 Kings Cross to Bradford crossing the LNWR 'Leeds New Line' at Howden Clough behind 61230 on 6 August 1960.   *(M. Mitchell)*

J39 0-6-0 No 64907 restarts from Batley with the 2.18pm Kings Cross to Bradford Exchange on 16 July 1955.
(D. Holmes)

A similar view with a Wakefield to Bradford dmu pulling away from the Great Northern island platform. Only the LNWR main line (the double track to the right of the signal box) is still in use today.
(M. Mitchell)

Travelling in the opposite direction this class 111 twin powered Metro Cammell set has departed Batley for Dewsbury Central and Wakefield Westgate, July 1962.
(Peter Sunderland)

Railmotor No 8 calls at Chickenley Heath in 1906. The view is towards Batley.

Earlsheaton looking towards Dewsbury. The architecture is similar to contemporary stations at Eccleshill, Idle and Shipley.

Upper Batley looking towards Dewsbury. The permanent station dated from 1866, when the original temporary facilities were used to construct Howden Clough. The main building is now a private house.

Batley looking north in early 1963. The Great Northern platform is the island on the right. The station is still open with just the two main LNWR platforms. The main building survives in non-railway use.
(Roger Hepworth)

The remains of Batley Carr station looking south in 1964 towards the 161 yard tunnel under the LNW line.
(Roger Hepworth)

N1 0-6-2T No 69471 approaching Dewsbury Central from Wakefield about 1955. Dewsbury Junction signal box is just visible between the engine and the signal post. *(A.M. Ross)*

Flushdyke Station looking towards Wakefield. It closed in 1941.

J50 0-6-0T No 68916 attacks the 1 in 50 grade between Batley and Shaw Cross with the Wrenthorpe pick up in 1954. *(A.M. Ross)*

The island platform at Ossett looking towards Dewsbury in 1961. Dating from 1889, this replaced the 1864 station with side platforms, a short distance towards Wakefield. *(Peter E Baughan)*

J50 No 69837 shunting the early afternoon down pick up goods in Ossett up yard in May 1961. Ossett closed for goods on 8 August 1964, four weeks before the passenger closure.   *(Roger Hepworth)*

The crew of 73168 wait the "right-away" from Ossett with the 11.40 Bradford Exchange to Kings Cross in July 1963.   *(Roger Hepworth)*

Tramway competition The Dewsbury & Ossett Tramway functioned from 12 November 1908 until 19 October 1933. Trams ran up to every 10 minutes on two routes which shared the 1 in 12 climb out of Dewsbury Market Place. One went to Ossett via Chickenley Heath and the other to Earlesheaton where No 6 has just arrived.

Closed to rail traffic in 1965, the 179 yard Earlesheaton Tunnel was restored and reopened in January 2013 as part of the Dewsbury to Ossett Greenway. It is now possible to walk or cycle from Headfield Junction across the viaducts on page 63 to Dewsbury Junction, then along the Wakefield line as far as Runtlings Junction and finally a short way towards Chickenley Heath.

(Roger Hepworth)

2 – 6 – 0 No 62065 bringing an eight coach excursion for Scarborough into Ossett on Whit Sunday 1961. More than eight coaches would have required double heading between Bradford and Wakefield. Ossett hadn`t had regular Sunday trains since 1951 and would have closed on Saturday 5 September 1964. Except that day there was a races special to Redcar hauled by 61115 and 45694 "Bellerophon" which returned after 2.00am on the Sunday morning.

(Roger Hepworth)

A Bradford Exchange to Wakefield Westgate DMU has just left Ossett. 51430 brings up the rear of the four coach set comprising two Metro Cammell power twins, later designated class 102.

(Roger Hepworth)

Alverthorpe looking towards Wakefield.

N1 0-6-2T No 69453 rounds the curve between Wrenthorpe West and South Junctions with a local from Bradford to Wakefield via Dewsbury. *(G.M. Staddon/N.E. Stead Collection)*

B1 4-6-0 No 61013 'Topi' pulling away from Wakefield Westgate with a Cleethorpes to Bradford Exchange working on 9 July 1966. *(N.E. Stead)*

The Methley Joint Railway

Fairburn 2-6-4T No 42073 (now preserved on the Lakeside & Haverthwaite Railway) calls at Ardsley with the 1.52pm (Saturdays Only) Castleford Central to Leeds Central on 5 November 1960. *(D. Holmes)*

By an Act of 21 July 1863, the Bradford, Wakefield & Leeds Railway was authorised to change its name to the West Yorkshire Railway. The same Act authorised a branch from a triangular junction north of Lofthouse to join both the North Eastern and Lancashire & Yorkshire Railways at Methley. Running powers were granted to the West Yorkshire Railway over the North Eastern to Castleford.

The North Eastern and Lancashire & Yorkshire didn't like this intrusion into their territory and the West Yorkshire could not afford to build the new line on its own. Therefore, by the Methley Railway Act 1864, it was arranged that the three companies should build the line at joint expense and that it should be administered by a joint committee to which each company would appoint two members.

The five-mile branch opened to goods in June 1865 but there was no regular passenger service until 1 May 1869 when the Great Northern Railway introduced one between Leeds Central and Castleford.

A service between Wakefield Westgate and Castleford began on 1 May 1876 by which time block signalling had been introduced on the Methley Joint and branch platforms had been provided at Lofthouse station. For a time this was known as

Lofthouse Joint but from 1888 until closure in 1960 it was Lofthouse & Outwood.

At its east end, the Methley Joint crossed over the Midland Main Line (just north of Altofts & Whitwood station) then crossed over the Methley Junction to Castleford route of the North Eastern Railway. It then came to Methley High Level Junction where it bifurcated passing through separate pairs of platforms in Methley Station. The south curve descended to join the North Eastern at Methley Joint Junction. The north curve joined the Lancashire & Yorkshire Railway at the confusingly named Lofthouse Junction. To the L&Y this was the junction for the line leading to Lofthouse. At Lofthouse itself, there were three junctions called Lofthouse North, South and East effecting the connection with the Leeds to Wakefield line.

Methley Station, on the Joint Line was the third one to serve that township. Very close but at a lower level, was Methley Junction on the Lancashire & Yorkshire Railway. The Midland Railway had a Methley Station over a mile to the north. British Railways tried to clarify the situation in the early 1950s by giving the suffix North to the Midland Station and South to that on the Joint Line. The L&Y Methley Junction had closed in 1943. North and

Methley South looking towards Leeds. The Castleford line is in the foreground. The other tracks lead to the junction with the Lancaster & Yorkshire Railway.
(Geoffrey Lewthwaite)

N1 No 69450 calls at Methley South with the 2.45pm Leeds Central to Castleford Central on 29 December 1956.
(D. Holmes)

V2 2-8-2 No 60977 passing Castleford Central in May 1959 with an express travelling towards York. The box and semaphore signals survived until 1997. One of the posters depicts Dixon of Dock Green advertising the Highway Code. *(Peter Sunderland)*

South then closed in 1957 and 1960 respectively.

The local passenger service over the Methley Joint was operated by the Great Northern Railway. In 1910 there were six trains per day, Mondays to Fridays from Leeds Central to Castleford and five from Wakefield Westgate to Castleford. The frequency was enhanced slightly on Saturdays but reduced on Sundays.

The final LNER timetable for Winter 1947/8 shows a better service from Leeds with ten departures Mondays to Fridays, eleven Saturdays but none on Sundays. From Wakefield Westgate there was just one to Castleford at 7am with no return working.

There were two other rail services between Leeds and Castleford. The North Eastern ran from Leeds New via Garforth to Castleford Central. That service ceased in 1951. The Lancashire & Yorkshire Railway went from Leeds Wellington to Castleford Cutsyke.

When diesel multiple units were introduced in 1957, the Methley Joint gained its best ever service with trains at almost hourly intervals between Leeds Central and Castleford Central, most of them continuing to Pontefract Monkhill and Baghill. These lasted only until October 1964 when the Methley Joint closed to passengers.

There remained a handful of peak hour trains between Leeds City and Castleford Cutsyke – successors to the one time L&Y service. These were diverted to Castleford Central in 1968 and have since been increased to a half hourly frequency.

Observant travellers should be able to spot the abutments of the Methley Joint bridge and then the site of Methley Joint Junction as their train rounds the curve between Methley and Whitwood Junctions.

The Methley Joint closed to all traffic, west of the Newmarket Silkstone Colliery branch, in April 1965. The connection from Methley High Level Junction to the North Eastern closed in 1967 but, until February 1981, coal traffic kept open the section from the Colliery eastward to the L&Y connection at Lofthouse Junction (Methley).

These cloth capped gentlemen are hopefully going to exercise some care before crossing the track at Stanley. *(J.C.W. Halliday)*

Two JC 0-C-0s, 04222 and 04208 head a special through Stanley on 21 September 1958. The gas lamps have been modernised since the 1957 view on page ??. *(D. Butterfield/N.E. Stead Collection)*

Stanley looking towards Castleford. From 1948 until 1952, the large building on the up platform was the home of Station Master Frank Kipling who we shall meet on page 71. The site has been totally redeveloped but further east a 1½ mile stretch of the former railway is now part of the Trans Pennine Trail.

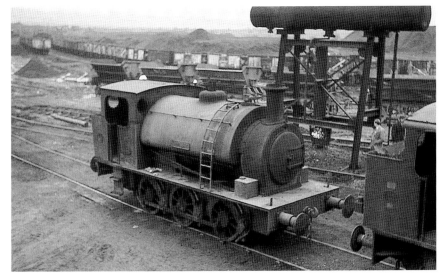

The eastern section of the Methley Joint was kept open until 1981 by Newmarket Colliery, which had its own internal system. Seen in March 1969, 0 - 6 - 0ST "Jubilee" was built by Hunslet in 1935.

(Martin Bairstow collection)

D5177 (later 25027) passing Methley South with coal from Newmarket on 31 July 1970. Since the photo on page 59 (top) taken in 1960, the signal box has had its frame renewed and steps moved to the far end. It closed in August 1970, after which the points were hand operated.

(M Mitchell)

Locomotives On Shed

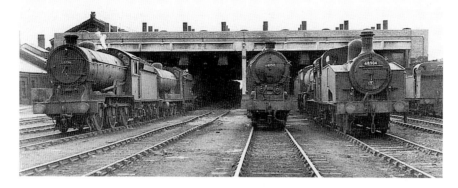

Two J39 0-6-0s 64796 and 64757 outside Ardsley Shed. To their right is No 68904, a 0-6-0T of Class J50 which were known as Ardsley tanks. The shed closed in October 1965.
(N.E. Stead Collection)

Copley Hill Shed stood within the triangle of lines between Holbeck, Wortley South and West Junctions. It was the Great Northern depot for Leeds and was home to main line passenger locos. A more humble ex GN Class J6 No 64277 is seen by the coaling stage. Copley Hill closed in September 1964.
(D. Butterfield/N.E. Stead Collection)

Hammerton Street (originally called Bowling) was the Great Northern shed for Bradford from 1876. N1 No 69443 is seen by the coaling stage in early BR days. After 1954, the shed was converted to maintain diesel multiple units and shunters. It closed in May 1984. *(N.E. Stead Collection)*

The 1882 Agreement

The Calder Viaduct on the Headfield Junction to Dewsbury Junction link during its first period of disuse in 1957.
(A.M. Ross)

The Spen Valley towns of Heckmondwike, Liversedge and Cleckheaton had been served by the Lancashire & Yorkshire Railway since 1849. There was a feeling, in the locality, that they would only get an adequate service to London if the Great Northern Railway were to reach them direct. Between 1871 and 1881, the GNR received written memorials and then actual deputations from the Spen Valley urging that an extension be built from Dewsbury.

Finally the GNR surveyed a route from just north of Dewsbury, through Heckmondwike, Liversedge, Cleckheaton and then on to Halifax. This would have paralleled the Lancashire & Yorkshire Railway virtually the whole way. In 1882 the GNR deposited a Bill in Parliament for the Dewsbury to Cleckheaton part of the scheme. In evidence before Parliament, the L&Y argued that considerable expense would be avoided if they and the GNR simply built a handful of short connecting lines between their two systems and arranged an exchange of running powers. This they agreed to do.

(1) The GN to build a short link from Hare Park, on the West Riding & Grimsby, to Crofton West Junction on the L&Y Knottingley to Wakefield line. This would give direct access from Doncaster to the Calder Valley route at Wakefield Kirkgate. The L&Y to have running powers over the GNR from Crofton to Doncaster.

(2) The GNR to rebuild the Pudsey branch so as to give a direct route from Leeds towards Dudley Hill and to build a line from Dudley Hill to Low Moor. The L&Y to have running powers from Leeds to Low Moor by this route.

(3) The GNR to build ½ mile link between Headfield Junction,

on the L&Y Dewsbury Market Place branch, and Dewsbury Junction, south of Dewsbury Central. This would give access from Dewsbury Central to the L&Y Calder Valley and Spen Valley Lines.

(4) The L&Y to build a south curve at Low Moor giving direct access from Cleckheaton towards Halifax. The GNR to have running powers from Crofton West Junction to Halifax both via Brighouse and via Cleckheaton.

It took until 1893 for all these connections to be completed.

The Headfield Branch

The ½ mile branch was authorised by an Act of August 1883. Virtually the entire project was built on embankments or viaducts including one of 14 spans. Maximum gradient was 1 in 55 climbing towards Dewsbury. The double track opened for goods traffic in October 1887. No regular passenger train ran over it until December 1893.

Following withdrawal of the circular service in August 1914, the Headfield branch carried little traffic and was closed completely in May 1933. The embankment and viaducts remained in situ and the line was eventually re-laid as a single track, reopening for goods traffic on 15 February 1965. This coincided with closure of the route between Drighlington, Dewsbury Central and Wakefield. It enabled a link to be maintained from Dewsbury GN goods depot direct to the Marshalling Yard at Healey Mills, on the ex L&Y Calder Valley Main Line.

Dewsbury goods depot closed in 1989, since when the Headfield branch has stood derelict again.

The Pudsey Loop

N1 0-6-2T No 69483 entering Pudsey Lowtown with the 12.25 Leeds Central to Bradford Exchange on 30 January 1954.   *(M. Goodall)*

The Leeds, Bradford & Halifax Junction Railway had missed Pudsey so as to avoid even steeper gradients. The town centre stands just over 1/2 mile from Stanningley station but at a higher level.

A branch line was authorised by the GNR Act of 24 July 1871 to commence at both Stanningley and Bramley. A contract was awarded for construction of the line in February 1875. The formation was built for double track. There were three underbridges and seven overbridges in the 1 3/4 miles from Stanningley to Pudsey Greenside. In the interest of economy only a single track was built initially, whilst no track at all was laid on the branch from Bramley.

Goods traffic began during the summer of 1877. A passenger service of 15 trains each way, weekdays only, began on 1 April 1878, starting from a bay platform at Stanningley. The intermediate station at Pudsey Lowtown was on a 1 in 50 gradient and the Government Inspector would not sanction its opening on a single line. Trains began to stop at Lowtown from 1 July 1878 by which time it had been equipped with a second platform, loop line and catch point.

The branch was worked by staff and ticket until it was doubled later on.

Extension of the Pudsey branch came as a result of the 1882 accord between the GNR and the Lancashire & Yorkshire Railway. Due to financial constraints, it was not until 1893 that work was completed. The extension took two forms. First the

A class 110 'Calder Valley' dmu pulls away from Pudsey Greenside bound for Bradford in May 1964. The main buildings are at a strange angle because they follow the original terminal alignment. A rake of excursion coaches is stabled in the yard.

(Peter Sunderland)

4 – 4 – 0WT No 507 arrives at Pudsey Lowtown with a service for Bradford Exchange. The loco was built in 1874 for use on Kings Cross suburban but later migrated north. The tank was under the coal bunker.

Pudsey Lowtown box (left) was original from 1878, although the 15 lever frame was replaced by one of 20 levers to accommodate the changes of 1893. These were more fundamental at Greenside (right) where a new 30 lever box was built on the through line. By 1961, both boxes were open only as required for access to the sidings. Otherwise, block working was from Bramley to Cutlers Junction.

(Mick York/ Richard Pulleyn collection)

branch was transformed into a loop off the main Leeds to Bradford line. In addition it was connected to the Dudley Hill to Low Moor line dealt with in the next chapter.

Track was laid from Bramley but no junction was created where it met the existing line from Stanningley as this was disconnected at the Pudsey end and used as a siding. From Pudsey Greenside, the line was extended through a 618 yard tunnel then along a very high embankment to join the Ardsley to Laisterdyke line at Cutlers Junction.

In 1910 there were some 24 trains each way on the Pudsey Loop but the service was anything but regular. Some trains were through from Leeds Central to Bradford Exchange, others from Leeds Central to Pudsey Greenside and some from Bramley to Bradford Exchange. At times it was necessary to change at Bramley to get from Leeds to Pudsey.

There had, since 4 June 1908, been an electric tram service from Leeds to Pudsey, less comfortable than the trains and slower but much more frequent and to a more central terminus in Pudsey. The GNR did nothing whatever to respond to this competition.

The 1922 timetable still shows the effect of wartime cuts. There were 14 scheduled passenger trains each weekday eastbound, and 17 westbound, the majority being through from Leeds Central to Bradford Exchange. There was no service round the Pudsey loop on a Sunday.

The summer 1938 service was only marginally better, still with no Sunday trains.

From 14 June 1954, the branch was served by Derby Lightweight diesel multiple units. Unlike the basic half hourly service via Stanningley, the Pudsey branch trains were not at regular intervals. The average frequency was about hourly but slightly erratic. All were through from Leeds Central to Bradford Exchange usually calling also at Armley Moor, Bramley and Laisterdyke which were missed by nearly all the direct trains via Stanningley.

The Pudsey Loop was an early casualty of the Beeching Report. At the TUCC hearing BR claimed that traffic had risen with the diesels but had then fallen back. From 1961 some off peak trains were withdrawn. By 1963 there were about 220 passengers a day in total at the two Pudsey stations. They closed on 13 June 1964. Three weeks later the branch closed completely. Armley Moor, Bramley and Laisterdyke were then served by a handful of trains via Stanningley until they succumbed on 2 July 1966. Stanningley itself closed on 30 December 1967 but only after a new station had been built to serve the Pudsey area.

B1 4-6-0 No 61034 'Chiru' and 'Black Five' No 44695 pause at Pudsey Greenside with an excursion from Bradford to Cleethorpes on 30 May 1964.
(D. Holmes)

A project unfinished

Commissioned at the same time as the Pudsey Loop in 1893, the additional pair of tracks between Wortley West and Bramley were known originally as the "branch" lines but were later re-designated "goods". They never carried that much traffic. Almost all Pudsey trains stopped at Armley and Bramley so had to use the main lines as there were no platforms on the "goods".

John Whitaker has supplied evidence that the GN actually started work on island platforms to be accessed by footbridge at Armley and subway at Bramley. The tracks were spaced to accommodate the intended platforms, which for reasons unknown were never completed. If they had been, then stopping trains to Pudsey could have been routed clear of faster GN and L&Y trains all the way from Wortley West. Instead, the extra lines were of value only in allowing slow goods trains to be overtaken. They were eventually taken out of use prior to the July 1969 re-signalling which saw closure of Wortley West, Armley and Bramley boxes.

At both Wortley West and Bramley, the junctions were equipped with facing point locks making the "goods" lines available for passenger trains.

Pudsey – Dudley Hill – Low Moor

A principal objective of the 1882 agreement with the Lancashire & Yorkshire Railway had been to achieve a more direct route from Leeds to the Spen Valley towns of Cleckheaton, Liversedge and Heckmondwike.

This was done by means of a curve from Tyersal Junction, 1½ miles west of Pudsey Greenside, to Broad Lane Junction, ¾ mile north of Dudley Hill. Between Broad Lane and Dudley Hill, the track was quadrupled so traffic from Pudsey direction could continue independently through separate platforms at Dudley Hill then dive under the Drighlington line in order to reach Low Moor. Here there was a junction with the Lancashire & Yorkshire Railway, just north of the station. There was also a separate GNR goods depot.

From 1 December 1893, a circular passenger service was introduced jointly by the GNR and Lancashire & Yorkshire Railways. Trains travelled from Leeds Central via Bramley, Pudsey Lowtown and Greenside, Dudley Hill, Low Moor, the Spen Valley, Thornhill, Dewsbury Central, Batley, Tingley and Beeston in order to regain Leeds Central 1 1/2 hours and 30 miles later. The service began with seven trains one way round and six the other. The 13 trains were worked 9 by the GNR and 4 by the L&YR which more or less reflected their respective shares of the route mileage.

This gave the three Spen Valley towns their direct service to Leeds but it was eclipsed in 1900 when the London & North Western Railway opened its 'Leeds New Line'. This offered a much shorter route from the three towns into Leeds albeit that the LNWR station at Cleckheaton was inconveniently sited. By 1910 the circular service was down to three trains each way, two on Sundays. This represented the entire passenger service over the Dudley Hill to Low Moor line. Other parts of the route saw a variety of other trains.

The circular service was withdrawn at the end of August 1914, leaving the Dudley Hill to Low Moor section without any passenger trains. It was singled during 1917 to release track for the war effort. It closed completely in May 1933. The GN goods shed at Low Moor survives in non-railway use but is no longer visible from passing trains. Low Moor station (L&Y) closed in 1965 but a long planned replacement may finally be on the way.

The original Dudley Hill station was nearer and in similar style to Birkenshaw, at Shetcliffe Lane level crossing. The Pudsey to Low Moor scheme relocated it to the junction. The street level entrance was through a hexagonal booking hall, from which steps emerged down to the four platforms. The two outer platforms each had a substantial stone building with a wooden one on the central island. All had projecting canopies. In the 1930s, there were around 17 stopping trains in each direction at anything but regular intervals. The station was closed on Sundays.

Earthworks were built for a direct Birkenshaw to Low Moor curve south of Dudley Hill, but it was never completed.

2 – 6 – 4T No 42141 climbs the 1 in 50 towards Dudley Hill with the 8.52 Bradford to Cleethorpes on Saturday 8 August 1964. The up goods loop is still in use but the up and down branch lines (Pudsey – Low Moor) have gone.   *(M Mitchell)*

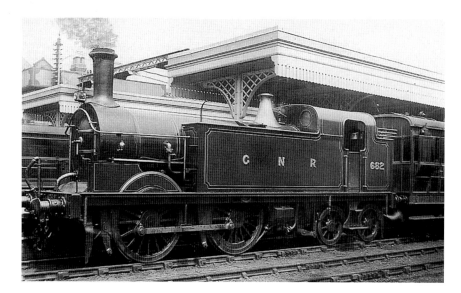

0-4-4T, No 682, seen at Leeds Central, was one of 16 'West Riding Tanks' built at Doncaster between 1881 and 1885.
(Martin Bairstow Collection)

Dating from 1893, Dudley Hill box had 65 levers, reduced to 51 after the Low Moor line closed. It was originally called Dudley Hill Yard to distinguish it from the 20 lever Station box, which lasted only from 1893 until 1924. There were once five tracks between Dudley Hill and Broad Lane Junction with an up goods loop between the two pairs. Signalman Mick York is seen working the box in the early 1960s. It closed in March 1968.
(Mick York/ Richard Pulleyn collection)

Batley to Beeston

Tingley Viaduct carried the Batley to Beeston branch over the Leeds to Wakefield main line. A class V2 2-6-2 is in charge of a London express.
(A.M. Ross)

A landmark on the line between Wakefield and Leeds is the tall five arch viaduct under which trains pass shortly after emerging from Ardsley Tunnel. There hasn't been anything on top of this structure since 1953. It stands as a monument to yet another Great Northern branch, built at no small expense to compete with an earlier railway already providing a direct link, in this case, from Leeds to Batley and Dewsbury.

As today's express speeds towards Leeds, one can look up to the right and see the disused formation curving off the viaduct and sweeping down to join the main line more than a mile to the north at what was Beeston Junction. Look even more closely before reaching Beeston Junction and you can see the abutments of a bridge which used to carry the Leeds bound track back across the main line so as to join it on the left hand side.

The Batley to Beeston route was authorised in 1881 but no work was undertaken until the Summer of 1887 apart from the relatively easy first half mile

between Batley West Junction and Soothill Wood Colliery. This section opened to coal traffic in the Autumn of 1887.

The flying junction at Beeston was not part of the original scheme but was authorised later by an Act of July 1889.

The route was in two parts: From Batley West Junction to Tingley West and from Tingley East to Beeston Junction. Earthworks were heavy with deep cuttings, high embankments, ten underbridges, the five arch, 62 feet high viaduct over the main line and the 659 yard tunnel at Soothill. There was an intermediate station at Woodkirk. Tingley Station was rebuilt on the same site in anticipation of the new route opening.

Goods traffic began on 1 July 1890. Two quarries were sited to the north west of Woodkirk. These gained a rail connection in 1892. There was a maximum gradient of 1 in 33 on the internal quarry system.

The passenger service commenced on 1 August

1890 with six trains each way between Leeds Central and Dewsbury Central. From November 1890 some trains ran in a circle from Leeds via Batley, Dewsbury, Ossett and back to Leeds via Wrenthorpe and Ardsley. L&Y trains ran from Leeds Central to Barnsley Exchange via Beeston, Batley and Dewsbury Central, then via Headfield Junction to reach Horbury & Ossett.

From 1 December 1893, the Batley to Beeston route was used by the joint GN/L&Y service mentioned in the previous chapter which made a circuit from Leeds Central via Pudsey, the Spen Valley, Dewsbury and back to Leeds.

Looking at the 1910 timetable, the GNR offered up to 17 weekday trains between Leeds Central Batley and Dewsbury. What was so complicated was where they went after Dewsbury.

The 6.32am from Leeds arrived Dewsbury at 6.58. After a quick turn round it left at 7.04 for Leeds Central via Drighlington and Pudsey. The 8.45am from Leeds appears to have no return working from Dewsbury.

By 1938, the service was reduced. Gone was the circular route via Cleckheaton, the Barnsley trains and the Sunday service. Mondays to Fridays, there were ten departures from Leeds to Dewsbury, most going on to Wakefield Westgate or coming back to Leeds via Ossett and Wrenthorpe.

Woodkirk station closed on 23 September 1939. The LNER timetable for Winter 1947/8 shows just six trains from Leeds Central, all through to Wakefield

	Departures from Leeds Central	Ultimate Destination
	5.15 am	Wakefield Westgate
	6.32	Dewsbury Central
	8.45	Dewsbury Central
	8.55	Barnsley
	9.09	Leeds Central via Ossett
	10.45	Leeds Central via Cleckheaton
	11.55	Leeds Central via Ossett
	12.20 pm	Ossett
	2.13	Barnsley
	2.35	Wakefield Westgate
	4.15	Leeds Central via Cleckheaton
	5.40	Leeds Central via Cleckheaton
	6.35	Ossett
	7.00	Barnsley
	8.25	Leeds Central via Ossett
TuThSO	9.35	Ardsley via Ossett
TuSX	10.30	Leeds Central via Ossett
TuThSO	10.58	Ossett
SUNDAYS		
	8.25 am	Leeds Central via Cleckheaton
	12.05 pm	Dewsbury Central
	4.25	Leeds Central via Cleckheaton
	8.35	Ossett

Westgate. There is an extra on Saturdays but only five trains the other way and nothing on Sundays.

The remaining passenger service over the Batley to Beeston line was withdrawn in October 1951. The line closed completely in July 1953 except between Woodkirk and Tingley. This section remained open until 1964 to serve the quarries at Woodkirk.

Woodkirk Station looking towards Tingley in August 1961.   *(M. Mitchell)*

Relief Station Master

In 1993 I was privileged to meet retired Station Master Frank Kipling at his home at Thornhill. He was then aged 86. He died in1994.

Frank George Kipling joined the Great Northern Railway shortly before his sixteenth birthday in 1922. His first appointment was as a lad messenger at City Road Goods Depot, Bradford.

He quickly trained as a booking clerk and moved to Great Horton Station in 1923 thus beginning the long progression up the clerk's scale which gave annual increments to the age of 31.

The neighbouring station at Horton Park did not employ a clerk, just porters under a station master. The Horton Park Station Master spent a lot of time in a sweet shop at the other side of Horton Park Avenue. One day he eloped with the lady from the sweet shop possibly absconding with both the station and shop takings. The LNER cut its losses (or possibly began to recover them) by abolishing the post of station master at Horton Park and placing it under Great Horton.

Frank Kipling was sent to cover the booking office at Horton Park. He reorganised the ticket rack, moving it nearer to the window. Then they sent Charlie Cook, a trainee clerk straight from school, who was too small to reach the rack in its new position so Frank made some steps for him out of old drawers.

There was a milk traffic from Cullingworth and Wilsden to Great Horton and Horton Park. The empties returned from Horton Park at 3.28 in the afternoon. This departure was often witnessed by children from local 'posh houses' with their nursemaids.

Once Charlie Cook was trained, Frank moved back to Great Horton. In 1926, he was living in a cottage near Duckett's crossing, between Hillfoot Tunnel and Laisterdyke. In order to get to work, he walked along the track to Laisterdyke Station where he caught a train changing at St Dunstans. One morning he encountered a headless corpse on the track which he duly reported on arrival at Laisterdyke. Nobody there was interested as their responsibility ended at the bridge carrying the Shipley branch - 'try Pudsey', they said.

Pudsey claimed that the body lay within the jurisdiction of Stanningley Station. Stanningley tried to throw responsibility back on to Pudsey but eventually persuaded to send staff to deal with it.

Frank decided that it might be easier in future to take the slightly longer route by road but one morning he stumbled upon the body of a man who had shot himself near Thornbury Cricket Field. After that he tried walking the other way by footpath through Tyersal, south of the railway line. But accidents come in threes, as Frank discovered when he found police fishing a body out of a quarry alongside his new walking route.

From Great Horton, Frank transferred to Dudley Hill Goods Yard which was particularly busy at this time with materials arriving for the building of the housing estate at Holmwood. Cement came from Ellesmere Port, slates from Blaenau Ffestiniog and window frames from Nottinghamshire.

After a spell on both goods and passenger work at Dudley Hill, Frank Kipling moved on to Laisterdyke where he was to remain for most of the 1930s.

He did have a period lodging at South Elmsall where he was also in charge of Hampole Station which despatched a lot of peas.

Whilst sitting in the booking office at Laisterdyke, Frank received a telephone call from one of the signal boxes instructing him to call an ambulance because the train recording lad had got a signal lever up his (posterior). After some protest, Frank was prevailed upon to carry out the instruction and

The northbound 'Yorkshire Pullman' passing Ardsley on 28 June 1961 behind Class A3 No 60039 'Sandwich'.
(D. Holmes)

in due course the lad was carried down the signalbox steps. Apparently there had been three levers pulled over. The lad had attempted to leap frog over the middle one using the two outer ones for support. He lost his grip with dire consequences. The damage was not permanent. During the subsequent Second World War, the lad rose to the rank of lieutenant commander in the Royal Navy. When he was demobbed afterwards, the LNER offered him his job back as a porter but he was not satisfied with that and failed to take up the invitation.

Frank was still booking tickets at Laisterdyke at the start of the Second World War. An enemy aircraft hit a wagon of butter in Quarry Gap sidings with an incendiary bomb setting the place alight and making it a target for further attack. Staff in the yard tried to get an engine to shunt the blazing wagon under the water column but they were attacked with machine gun fire. They all took refuge under Dick Lane bridge apart from Yard Inspector Harry England who was deaf and oblivious to the danger.

Cutlers Junction signalbox lost its toilet in the raid. Shrapnel passed through Laisterdyke East box where Joseph Kipling, Frank's father was on duty.

At West Box, which stood on a gantry, the steps were blown off leaving signalman Cyril Wattam marooned. When the Box was hit again, he had to shin down an adjacent telegraph pole with injury to his hands.

Frank himself was not far from danger as a bomb exploded outside the booking office. The ticket rack was destroyed. Tickets ended up everywhere including along the up platform and Frank spent the next day, Sunday gathering them up and sorting them out.

Rails were twisted and traffic was interrupted over the remainder of the weekend but trains were running again on Monday, a platelayer's cabin deputising for the damaged West Box.

The roof over the staircase onto the down platform had been blown off and was never restored.

In 1942, Frank Kipling was appointed a relief station master nominally based at Ardsley though he continued to live in Bradford. The LNER had other relief station masters based at Leeds, Bradford and Wakefield. Between them they covered for annual leave, sickness and any other vacancies at all LNER stations in the West Riding.

Sometimes the appointment might be for an odd day, sometimes a week, occasionally a fortnight. At that time station masters worked six days per week with a half day alternately mid week and on Saturdays. Inevitably, when planning a holiday, the regular man preferred to finish work on Saturday dinner time then have off the week which would have involved working Saturday afternoon. The relief man invariably got the worse deal.

Frank still has his note book recording all the stations he visited. The relief man could sometimes fall into a trap which the regular incumbent would have known to avoid. At Denholme, during the War, he was alerted by lady porter Amy to what she considered was a major embankment fire. It was all hands to the stirrup pump. This piece of machinery was not functioning too well and they got water everywhere. Amy had to adjourn to put her coat on but eventually they got the fire out. Then a platelayer appeared pleading that he had used two boxes of matches getting the fire going. He was trying to burn the vegetation by day because there had been problems with locomotives starting fires during the blackout.

A relief station master would expect to find things in reasonable order when he arrived at a station. On one of his very few visits to Ingrow, a Monday probably in August 1945, Frank found half the staff missing. By that time the LNER station master also had charge of the adjacent LMS station on the Worth Valley branch. On this occasion, the LMS clerk was on holiday, the porter was sick and

Joseph W. Kipling, Frank's father, was a signalman at Laisterdyke East from 1909 until 1941.

(*Frank Kipling Collection*)

'Black Five' 4-6-0 No 44951 passing Laisterdyke with an excursion heading towards Leeds at Whitsun
1966.   (D.J. Mitchell)

An ex North Eastern Railway G5 No 67311 pulls into Stanley with a Leeds Central to Castleford Central
train in February 1957.   (P.B. Booth/N.E. Stead Collection)

the station was being run by the LNER goods checker, an obliging chap who seemed to be enjoying himself booking passengers instead of his usual job.

The LNER porter signalman was also missing so Frank had to arrange for the two signalmen to go onto overtime so as to cover for the short middle turn which was normally done by the porter signalman. This man's other duties included cleaning the carriages which were stabled at Ingrow so Frank swept them out himself.

Nobody had thought to leave behind the key to the safe in the LMS booking office so Frank was unable to get at the previous day's takings. He was supposed to send these in a sealed leather bag to Keighley. Some time later, Frank received a demand from the internal audit department to explain why he had not forwarded Sunday's takings.

In March 1946, a request was received from the LNER at Cambridge for six relief station masters. The Leeds Area responded with the offer that they could spare just one - Frank Kipling - who was to spend two weeks at Wimblington, a place he had never heard of previously which was located just south of March on the line to St. Ives.

Arriving mid afternoon on the Monday, Frank sought digs and was lucky to bump into a chap who was able to fix him up at a local pub. His good fortune continued when he sat down to evening meal to find that food rationing had, apparently, failed to catch on in this part of the world. They went short of nothing.

The only commodity which was in limited supply was railway wagons for which every station seemed desperate. During Frank's stay, a train of empties left Whitemoor Yard, March, for Cambridge with 76 on but arrived just engine and brake after each intermediate station had succeeded in getting half a dozen into their yard.

The wagons were needed for loading straw and other farm produce. This needed bags which could be hired from the railway company subject to a complicated price structure with which the station master had to be familiar.

A relief station master could never win. If he was too conversant with local conditions, he was taunted as a 'know all'. If he had no idea then he was a 'know nowt'. Frank preferred the latter endearment so he concealed his previous experience with sacks and allowed his local staff the pleasure of imparting their knowledge upon him.

Frank's first permanent station was Stanley on the Methley Joint to which he moved in July 1948. His bedroom was above the down waiting room. The first train, at 5.20 in the morning, used to convey miners to Methley. On Monday mornings they would wake Mr and Mrs Kipling as they enthused noisily about Saturday's match at Wakefield Trinity. Frank would bang on the bedroom floor with his boot, and the porter would warn them that 't'boss would be after them'. When they returned in the early afternoon, they would apologise blaming the shortest one of their number for the disturbance.

Frank's job was to sell rail travel so he would visit the local Working Men's Club or Miners' Welfare to enquire about arrangements for the annual outing. Frank knew his customers' requirements and could offer a BG in the middle of the train where they could set up a bar. He would assure them that, whilst travelling by train to the seaside, it would be as if the Club had never closed. Then he could offer free first class returns to the Committee allowing them a preview trip to ensure satisfactory arrangements at the other end.

The station master at Stanley also had charge of Methley South as well as the sidings at New Market Colliery which was located between the two.

During the period January to March each year, Stanley despatched up to seven or eight wagons of rhubarb each day. An engine came from Ardsley with a brake van to pick up the loaded wagons which were taken to Doncaster. There they were shunted on to the front of the Aberdeen to London fish and meat train for delivery to Covent Garden next morning.

On Summer Saturdays, holiday and excursion trains used to amalgamate at Stanley. A portion would arrive (say) from Bradford via Dewsbury. The loco would propel the carriages back over the cross onto the up line then abandon them. The portion from Leeds would then arrive, propel back onto the other coaches, then continue with the full train bound for Bridlington or other holiday destinations. The station master had to make sure that the catch points were clamped on the up line west of the station. In the other direction, the operation was easier. The Leeds train would simply leave the Bradford carriages in Stanley platform until an engine came to rescue them. It is always a more simple operation to divide a loco hauled train than it is to amalgamate one.

Freight also used to divide at Stanley so that different portions could take the Ardsley and Lofthouse curves when they reached the end of the Methley Joint. On one occasion, a double headed freight arrived at 2am westbound (up direction). It proceeded to reverse over onto the down main to leave the rear portion in Stanley platform. The wagons would wait here until an engine came to take them forward. In the meantime they would block the down line but it was the middle of the night with no passenger traffic wanting to pass.

Unfortunately the two locos set off for Ardsley with their remaining half load so fast that they broke the coupling between the rear engine and the leading wagon. The train rolled back and was diverted by trap points into the yard, demolishing a gas lamp as it went. The rear of the train ended up the embankment.

Frank's first job was to find the stop tap for the gas lamp before he could contemplate allowing a steam locomotive near the scene especially as the train included paraffin tanks. There was a tow rope in the guards van which they attached to the engines and so removed the front vehicle which was loaded with ten tons of flour. They got this and the other wagons which were still on the track over onto the down side and into a siding. The 5.20 down passenger train was able to pass but they had to work to clear the up line for when it returned.

Only after the morning rush hour had passed did they get the breakdown train to tackle the vehicles which were off the road.

Promotion came in 1952 with a move to Ovenden with responsibility also for North Bridge and Holmfield.

The story continues in *Part Two*.

From the bombing raid until closure in 1966, Laisterdyke had an open staircase to the down platform and a covered one on the up side.

(John Bateman)

44693 passing Laisterdyke West box with the Bradford portion of the up "Yorkshire Pullman" in 1967

(D J Mitchell)

More on the Bradford Bombing Raids

Richard Pulleyn adds some detail to the bombing raid on Laisterdyke at which Frank Kipling was present.

There were five significant air raids on Bradford during World War II but the worst attack was the third which started at 10.13pm on Saturday 31 August 1940 and lasted until 2.40 the following morning. It was a warm, calm night and the cinemas had just closed, so there were crowds on the streets making their way home by bus, tram and train.

For four hours 30 German aircraft, thought to have been twinengined Heinkel 111s in relays of two, three or four, flew over the city dropping 47 high explosive bombs, 7 delayed action bombs, 11 oil incendiaries and 51 magnesium incendiaries.

One plane followed a goods train for a number of miles towards Bradford until the crew escaped by stopping in Stanningley Tunnel. When they set off again they found that Laisterdyke had been at the centre of a raid. It was thought that the Germans had been looking for the English Electric factory or for Birkshall gas works; the latter was hit, as was the gas works on Valley Road, but in neither case were the gas holders damaged.

At Laisterdyke, the West signal box was in an extremely exposed position on girders above the tracks. The signalman was provided with a steel cabinet in which to take refuge during an air raid, but while he was in there, the signal box received a direct hit from an incendiary bomb. When he emerged from the shelter he found that the box was well alight. It was not possible to use the wooden steps down to safety so he took the only remaining option which was to leap on to a nearby telegraph pole and slide down, severely injuring his hands in the process.

It is thought that the signal box was completely destroyed but a careful search of surviving LNER records at the National Archive in Kew has failed to reveal any reference to this significant attack. Contemporary reports were subject to heavy censorship. One national newspaper simply stated: The populace of a northeast town experienced some hours under air raid conditions. Damage was done in various parts of the town, but none of this can be remotely described as of military importance. A survey of the damage yesterday only emphasised the remarkable manner in which the town has escaped with such slight casualties. In reality, 49 major incidents were dealt with by over 3,000 army, police and emergency service personnel; one person died and 111 were injured during the raid.

Reports of the Railway Executive Committee provide some further information. In addition to damage to the signal box, three high explosive bombs fell on the Laisterdyke station area; the booking office was badly affected, with tickets strewn around the tracks and the Shipley line was blocked by an UXB (unexploded bomb). The railway reopened on Sunday 1 September with handsignalling from 3.10pm but trains were suspended again later that afternoon because of a further suspected UXB. The total interruption was 14½ hours.

During the fourth raid on Bradford, at 8.46pm on 14 March 1941, the railway was again one of the targets and Clayton signal box is reported to have been badly damaged. That was the night of the Leeds Blitz, sometimes referred to as the Quarter Blitz because, even that night, the scale was nothing like what was falling on Sheffield and Glasgow.

The Luftwaffe's final impact on Bradford occurred on 5 May 1941, when a plane was shot down, killing three residents when it crash landed on Idle High Street.

Manufactured by A J Riley of Batley, the air raid shelter was designed for industrial premises including signal boxes. *(Richard Pulleyn collection)*

The post war Laisterdyke West was a new box on the same girders. It lasted until June 1970.

Industrial Locomotives

When steam finished on British Railways in 1968, a number of enthusiasts found solace on colliery and other industrial lines where some quite ancient locomotives were still working.

With the subsequent decline of heavy industry, it is not just the engines but most of the industrial sites themselves which have become memories.

'St. Johns', seen at East Ardsley Colliery on 4 July 1964, was a 0-4-0 Peckett dating from 1922. The Colliery was served by a main line connection on the south west side between Ardsley loco shed and station.

(Martin Bairstow Collection)

Roundwood Colliery was reached by a short branch running to the south east between Alverthorpe and Flushdyke. Hudswell Clarke 0-6-0ST No 23 is seen in action at the Colliery on 12 May 1962.

(John Holroyd)

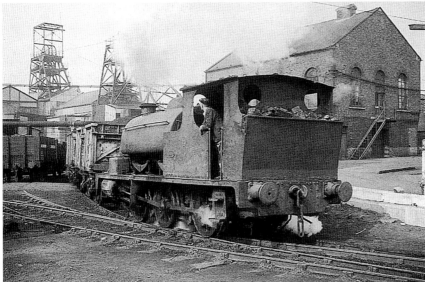

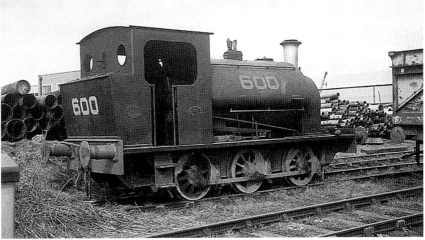

Cohens Foundry had a private siding at Stanningley on the north side of the main line. It made a level crossing with the Pudsey branch of Leeds City Tramways. Hunslet 0-6-0ST No 600 was photographed in 1964.

(Martin Bairstow Collection)

Bradford to London

B1 No 61161 approaching Adwalton Junction with the Bradford portion of the 10.50am from Kings Cross on 1 September 1962. The Batley line is on the right.   *(M Mitchell)*

Historically most London trains started as separate portions from Leeds Central and Bradford Exchange, combining at Wakefield Westgate. The arrangements there were rather labour intensive involving a pilot engine and a shunter. When the time came to eliminate the joining and splitting of trains, they cut the through service from Bradford, an affront to civic pride.

In 1887, the first express of the day left Leeds Central at 7.15am and stopped at Holbeck three minutes later for the connection from Harrogate. It was joined at Wakefield Westgate by the Bradford portion which had left Exchange at 7.00. This stopped at Laisterdyke for the Halifax connection, a GN train nonstop via Low Moor. It was then nonstop to Wakefield unless requested to take up London passengers at Morley or Ardsley. The combined train had the same conditional stops at Sandal and Hemsworth. It reached Doncaster at 8.01 and then continued with stops at Bawtry, Retford, Newark, Grantham, Essendine, Peterborough and Finsbury Park to arrive Kings Cross at 11.16.

The fastest train of the day was the "Dining Car Express" at 10.00 am from Leeds Central. Stopping only at Holbeck, Wakefield Westgate, Grantham and Peterborough, this reached Kings Cross in 3hrs 55mins. The Bradford portion left at 9.45 stopping only at

Ardsley unless a request were made to take up London passengers at Morley. There was also a through portion at 9.12 from Halifax stopping at Laisterdyke, Batley, Dewsbury and Ossett. This would also pick up London passengers at Hipperholme, Lightcliffe, Wyke, Low Moor, Dudley Hill and Birkenshaw. One assumes that actual stops at these places were comparatively rare or time keeping would have been impossible. The Halifax train reached Westgate at 10.04, the Bradford at 10.12, the Leeds at 10.18 and the whole thing departed at 10.21. There were no London trains from Leeds and Bradford on a Sunday.

The Dining Car on the 10.00 am from Leeds and 5.30 pm from Kings Cross had been introduced on 1 November 1879, the first such service in this Country. The "Prince of Wales" was built by the Pullman Company in Detroit, shipped in parts and reassembled at the Midland Railway works in Derby. First class passengers paid a supplement and rode in the coach the whole way. The kitchen was in an adjacent carriage.

As more restaurant cars appeared, it became the practice for first class passengers to make their way through the train at meal times. Third class restaurant cars were introduced in July 1896.

The "singles" (page 33) gave way to "Atlantics" on expresses between Kings Cross and Leeds. Built in 1898, No 990 "Henry Oakley" was the first 4 – 4 – 2 tender engine in the British Isles. Named after the Great Northern General Manager, it was the first of 22 of what became LNER class C2. "Atlantics" were superseded by 4 – 6 – 2 "Pacifics" in the 1930s, after the Calder Bridge at Wakefield had been strengthened to take the heavier six coupled engines. "Henry Oakley" was withdrawn in 1937 but preserved by the LNER. It is seen at Haworth on 8 July 1977. *(John Sagar)*

The GN had followed the Midland in having third class carriages on all trains from 1872. Previously, some expresses had been first and second class only. Second class was abolished on most of the GN, including the West Riding from 1 January 1886. Third class was redesignated second in 1956.

By 1910, the fastest Leeds to London time had come down to 3••• hours by the 2.00pm "Dining Car Express" which stopped only at Holbeck and Wakefield. The Bradford portion left at 1.25 with stops at Batley, Dewsbury and Ossett, plus the now familiar requests at Laisterdyke, Dudley Hill, Birkenshaw, Upper Batley, Earlsheaton and Flushdyke.

There was now a service on Sundays, including the "Luncheon Car Express" at 10.50 from Leeds Central which reached London at 3.15. The Bradford portion left at 10.25 calling all stations via Morley except St Dunstans. Dudley Hill and Birkenshaw were by request only for London.

The First World War took its toll on both speed and frequency. The 2.00pm "flier" from Leeds was cancelled from mid February 1915. All GN restaurant cars were withdrawn in May 1916. They began to reappear from February 1919. In summer 1922, the fastest train was the 10.00am from Leeds Central which reached Kings Cross at 1.55pm with stops at Holbeck, Wakefield Westgate, Doncaster, Retford, Grantham and Peterborough. The Bradford portion left at 9.35 with stops at Batley, Dewsbury and Ossett and a conditional one at Birkenshaw.

On 27 September 1937, the LNER introduced the "West Riding Limited". All eight coaches, four articulated pairs in a special two tone blue livery, left Bradford Exchange at 11.10 am behind two N2 class

0–6–2Ts. At Leeds Central, an A4 "Pacific" came on to the other end for the 11.31 departure nonstop to Kings Cross which was reached at 2.15pm. The return was at 7.10pm, reaching Bradford in the same 3hrs 5mins. The formation included two kitchens, each occupying more than half a carriage, allowing both first and third passengers to be served at their seats. Two A4s were dedicated to the "West Riding Limited", 4495 "Golden Fleece" and 4496 "Golden Shuttle", named to convey an association with the Bradford wool trade. The train ran Mondays to Fridays until 31 August 1939, one of the first victims of the Second World War. No 4496 was renamed "Dwight D Eisenhower" in September 1945, after the Supreme Allied Commander who later became President of the United States.

In 1957, the fastest time from Leeds to London was 3hrs 22mins by the nonstop "Queen of Scots Pullman" at 4.40pm from Central. The fastest ordinary train was the "West Riding" at 7.50am which reached Kings Cross in 3hrs 54mins with stops at Holbeck, Wakefield Westgate and Doncaster. The Bradford portion left Exchange at 7.30 stopping at Morley. There were seven Bradford to London through trains in the course of the day.

12 minutes were allowed between the arrival of the Bradford portion and departure of the combined train. The Bradford coaches arrived in the up platform, where the loco was detached. The pilot engine came on the back and drew the train into up siding No 1. There the shunter raised the buckeye, shortened the buffers and removed the end board if there was one.

Then the "Pacific" arrived from Leeds. The shunter attended to the buckeye, buffers and end board before removing the tail lamp. He then signalled the Bradford portion to set back onto the main train. Once the buckeyes had engaged, he connected the steam heat, vacuum brakes and electrical jump leads. The Leeds guard made his way to the back of the train, part of which was still in the siding. Overseeing the operation was the peak capped station inspector who unlocked the gangway doors and hung the curtains between the newly coupled coaches. Satisfied that the operation was complete, carriage doors shut and departure time reached, he signalled to the guard and then relayed the guard's signal forward to the driver.

In the other direction, the combined train arrived in the down platform. The inspector removed the curtains and locked the gangway doors between the coaches to be split. The shunter climbed down to uncouple the vacuum and steam heat. The jumper leads were left to disconnect themselves. He then pulled the buckeye chain as the front portion moved half a coach length towards Leeds. He dropped the buckeye, extended the buffers and, if you were lucky, attached an end board. The guard put a tail lamp on and the Leeds train was ready to go.

The shunter then attended to the front end of the Bradford portion before the engine waiting in the down siding was signalled to back on.

There were two shunters employed at Westgate alternating between early and late turns. They were busiest on Summer Saturdays when trains to East Coast resorts also joined and divided. In 1964 there was a 7.22am from Bradford / 8.02 from Leeds to Great

Ex LMS "crab" No 42863 passing Howden Clough with the 12.20pm from Yarmouth Vauxhall to Bradford Exchange on Saturday 22 July 1961.   *(M Mitchell)*

4496 "Golden Shuttle" at Wakefield Westgate when new in 1937. It was withdrawn in 1963 as 60008 "Dwight D Eisenhower" and donated to the National Railroad Museum, Green Bay, Wisconsin, USA.

"Black Five" No 44694 has arrived at Wakefield Westgate with the portion from Bradford. *(Roger Hepworth)*

The coaches have been pulled back into the up siding by a WD sent from Wakefield (L&Y) shed, not the usual station pilot. The Leeds portion has arrived and the WD is now propelling the Bradford coaches into the rear of the combined train.
(Roger Hepworth)

B1 4-6-0 No 61229 passing Earlsheaton in June 1957 with the 4.47pm through coaches from Bradford Exchange to Kings Cross. *(A.M. Ross)*

J39 0-6-0 No 64801 passing Runtlings Lane Junction with Bradford to Kings Cross through coaches in 1954. *(A.M. Ross)*

2 - 6 - 4T No 42085 at Wakefield Kirkgate on 18 July 1967, about to run round the through carriages from Halifax which it will take to Westgate and attach to the London train. The loco was withdrawn when steam finished in the West Riding on 1 October but is preserved on the Lakeside & Haverthwaite Railway. *(Roger Hepworth)*

Yarmouth. This called at Batley, Dewsbury and Ossett as did the 7.48/ 8.21 to Skegness. The Leeds portion called at Ardsley. The same applied to the 8.52/ 9.27 to Cleethorpes. These trains stopped at Dewsbury Central and Ossett on their last day, 5 September 1964.

After that, Bradford portions continued to run nonstop via Morley until July 1966 when they were diverted via Wortley West Junction. This enabled them to serve New Pudsey when it opened on 6 March 1967. Two months later, the joining of trains at Wakefield ceased on the closure of Leeds Central. From 1 May 1967, the Bradford portion ran to the east end of Leeds City before setting back into the main train standing in one of the through platforms. In the other direction, an engine came on the back and drew the rear four coaches to New Pudsey and Bradford Exchange. Some of these workings were steam hauled until 1 October 1967.

There was one exception. 1 May 1967 also saw a limited number of Deltic hauled eight coach trains which, for the first time in 28 years, restored the timings of the "West Riding Limited". Mondays to Fridays, the 7.00amfrom Bradford reached London at 10.05 stopping at New Pudsey and Wakefield Westgate. It was closely followed by the 7.30 nonstop from Leeds arriving Kings Cross at 10.13. These trains were later christened the "Bradford Executive" and "Leeds Executive".

Splitting at Leeds City finished in May 1971. Three times a day, all ten coaches went through to Bradford, often struggling behind a class 31 on the climb towards New Pudsey where the train was too long for the platform. At other times, Bradford passengers had to change onto a local DMU.The "Bradford Executive" still took the direct Wortley West to South curve. There was still one train joining at Wakefield Westgate. The 8.40am from Halifax started out with a class 31 diesel and three or four coaches. It had been a 2 6 – 4T prior to 1967. The loco ran round at Huddersfield and

again at Wakefield Kirkgate which was not a stop in the public timetable. At Wakefield Westgate it stopped in the down platform before drawing forward and setting back into the class 47 hauled train which had arrived from Leeds. The corresponding return working dropped the Halifax portion at Doncaster. It followed five minutes behind the Leeds train as far as Hare Park where it took the line to Kirkgate. It finished in May 1978 when fixed formation High Speed Trains began to appear. The full high speed service began in May 1979. Eight coach trains with a class 43 on each end were capable of 125 mph. The service was hourly with most trains taking less than 2••• hours from Leeds. Three a day went through to Bradford via Leeds in addition to the single direct one.

In May 1983, the northbound "Bradford Executive" was diverted via Leeds and the following year the southbound. This left the Wortley West to South curve with no regular passenger service much to the dismay of James Towler, Chairman of the Yorkshire Area Transport Users Consultative Committee. He maintained that a formal closure notice should have been published inviting users to submit objections to his Committee which could hold a public hearing and report to the Minister of Transport who would then authorise closure. BR said that diverting a train away from a short curve did not count as a closure under the 1962 Act.

Mr Towler found an ally in Bradford Council who had been complaining about the paucity of through London trains ever since the changes of 1971. They took BR to the High Court in April 1987 and won. BR appealed but lost at the Court of Appeal in December. They were then forced to publish a formal closure proposal inviting former users of the direct train to say what hardship they would suffer if the diversion were to become permanent. The statutory procedure was followed and the Minister confirmed closure.

Writing in Modern Railways (Feb 1988),Mr Towler claimed the episode to have been a triumph for rail users, BR having scored an own goal by their refusal to follow the correct procedure when first asked. What the case actually proved was that only withdrawal of the absolute last train triggers the closure procedure. When BR wanted to close the Stockport – Stalybridge line to passengers, they simply reduced the hourly service to one train a week in one direction only. And it's been like that for 25 years. So who scored the own goal?

Meanwhile Bradford Council had lost interest in the Wortley Curve. In October 1988, BR diverted the remaining Bradford through trains to Forster Square. The Council's attention turned to lobbying for electrification between Leeds and Bradford Forster Square. Surely this would increase the number of London trains. Airedale & Wharfedale electrification was completed in 1995 but it didn't bring any more Bradford to London trains.

There is now just one each way. On Mondays to Fridays it leaves Forster Square at 6.30am with stops at Shipley, Leeds and Wakefield Westgate to reach Kings Cross at 8.59. Departure from Leeds is at 7.00am making this the one train of the day to do the 185¾ miles in under two hours.

Since 2007, there has been a half hourly service from Leeds to Kings Cross. Most trains take about 2¼ hours and have connections from both Bradford Interchange and Forster Square.

But passengers don't like changing trains. About 1997, GNER, the first franchised operator, thought they'd found thesolution to this. Four times a day, they ran a bus from Bradford to connect with London trains at Wakefield Westgate. Patronage was almost nil.

The Bradford connection at Wakefield Westgate on 3 March 1997. John and I had it to ourselves.

(John Holroyd)

Ex Great Central C12 No 67444 is ready to draw the Bradford portion back into the up siding at Wakefield Westgate about 1950. The loco was withdrawn in 1957 after a life of 50 years.

The Drigh Bus

Based on an article by John Sykes in the October 2001 Journal of the LNER Study Group.

Amongst the large railway community at Ardsley, the term "bus" was applied to several local passenger services. In GN days, the "Chickenley Bus" was the steam railmotor on the Batley – Chickenley Heath Ossett line. After the Grouping, Ardsley took over working the "Barnsley Bus", the ex Great Central service from Wakefield Westgate. Not an Ardsley working but still on the GN, the Halifax High Level train was the "Pellon Bus". The longest surviving member of this select genre was the "Drigh Bus" which lasted until 11 June 1955, running basically between Ardsley and Drighlington & Adwalton with occasional extensions at either end.

The 1887 Working Timetable shows approximately 40 passenger trains in each direction stopping, passing or terminating at Drighlington. Most expresses went via Morley, only one via Batley. Conversely, most Bradford to Wakefield locals travelled via Batley, with only one via Morley. There were five trains from Bradford to Ardsley. Otherwise passengers for Gildersome, Morley and Tingley had to change at Drighlington, from where 11 trains started; eight to Ardsley, one to Wakefield via Morley and two via Batley.

These last two trains help explain the signs at Drighlington proclaiming "Change for Gildersome and Batley Branches". The Gildersome Branch is itself a curious term as Morley is by far the larger town. It presumably derives from the line being opened in two sections; Laisterdyke to Gildersome in 1856 and Gildersome to Ardsley the following year.

On Sundays, there were only a few through trains. The number increased in later years but there was never a Sunday Drigh Bus.

When the Batley – Tingley – Beeston Junction line opened on 1 August 1890, Drighlington gained a service to Leeds Central. The 1910 "Bradshaw" suggests there were 18 through trains in each direction between Bradford and Leeds but closer scrutiny shows that on most journeys, a change would be required at either Drighlington or Ardsley or both.

For example, the 9.25am from Bradford is shown as calling at all stations, except Dudley Hill and Birkenshaw, to Leeds via Ardsley. In fact, the 9.25 was a through train to Wakefield via Batley. It arrived Drighlington at 9.41 and any Leeds passengers had to change onto the 9.50 which started there for Wakefield via Morley. This called at Ardsley at 10.04, where persevering Leeds passengers could change onto the

The "Drigh Bus" in its final form. C12 No 67386 at Drighlington & Adwalton with a pair of push-pull fitted ex Great Central clerestory coaches. *(D Atkinson collection)*

10.09 to Leeds, which was from Castleford. Only three trains actually ran through from Bradford to Leeds via Tingley with four in the opposite direction.

The July 1923 WTT shows four through trains from Bradford to Leeds Central via Tingley. The service to Wakefield follows the previous pattern so local traffic via Morley is still mainly dependent on the Drigh Bus. 12 trains started from Drighlington, five to Ardsley, three to Lofthouse, largely for the benefit of mineworkers, two to Wakefield Westgate via Batley, one via Morley and one to Leeds via Tingley.

At this time, the Drigh bus was anything but a shuttle service. With the Saturday variations, it involved no fewer than 15 loco diagrams from four different sheds, most involving just one trip to Drighlington as part of the day's work.

The biggest contribution was from Ardsley shed with five A5 4 – 6 – 2Ts and two J3 or J4 goods engines. There were two N1s from Copley Hill and another two from Hammerton St, Bradford which also supplied three 4 – 4 2Ts of class C12. On Saturdays, an Ingrow based N1 came in to Drighlington at 2.37pm from Wakefield via Morley, then went light engine to Bradford.

Having arrived at Drighlington down platform, terminating trains would draw forward beyond the signal box. The engine would run round and could then either bring the train into the up platform or take refuge in the shunt siding. It would often have to do this as there would be a Bradford to Wakefield preceding its departure. The signal diagram confirms there was both track capacity and signalling to facilitate this.

The two 0 – 6 – 0 goods engines arrived Drighlington at 5.52am and 9.20pm, returning at 6.13am to Lofthouse and 9.52pm to Ardsley. Their use was in contravention of the main recommendation arising from the 1895 accident. On 25 July that year, a 0 – 4 – 2 tender engine arrived at Drighlington, ran round and was waiting in the up loop. The loco was now at the head of the train facing Ardsley tender first.

An excursion is booked to stop at Gildersome, five years after closure to regular passengers. This was a fairly common practice at closed stations in the pre-Beeching era.

The "Chickenley Bus" at Ossett between trips to and from Batley. Railmotors 7 and 8 were built in 1906. The locos had a streamline casing which was removed the following year.

A Bradford to Wakefield train was standing in the up platform when, for some reason, the 0 – 4 – 2 set off from the loop into the back of it.

The Report recommended either that unless a turntable were to be provided, only tank engines should be used on terminating trains. A driver has a much better view from a tank engine running bunker first than from a tender loco going tender first. In 1898, the first ten class C2 (LNERC12) 4 – 4 – 2Ts were allocated to the West Riding, possibly with this in mind.

The summer 1939 WTT shows nine trains starting from Drighlington, four to Ardsley, one to Lofthouse, three to Wakefield via Morley and one via Batley. On Saturdays only, the 4.50pm arrival from Leeds Central was rostered for a Sentinel railcar which returned to Ardsley at 5.38. This was a Copley Hill based car,

replaced by a conventional train on its usual Leeds – Castleford trip, where the Saturday traffic might have overwhelmed it.

By 1944, the number of trains was down to six. In September 1951, it reduced to just two. The early morning arrival from Wakefield via Batley returned at 6.44am to Ardsley. The 3.15pm from Wakefield via Morley, which didn't run on Saturdays, reached Drighlington at 3.43 and returned at 5.46pm. Regular motive power was a C12, usually 67386, with an ex Great Central two coach push – pull set.

The only other trains at Gildersome and Tingley were the 5.51 am Bradford to Wakefield and 6.09am the other way. Gildersome closed when the "bus" was withdrawn on 11 June 1955. Tingley had already closed on 3 January 1954, but a few expresses continued to serve Morley until the last day of 1960.

Gildersome looking towards Bradford with the main building at road level above the entrance to the 156 yard tunnel.

The ticket rack at Drighlington & Adwalton at 1.45pm on 21 November 1961. Of the 40 ticket types in issue, 11 appear to have done business so far that day.

(John Holroyd)

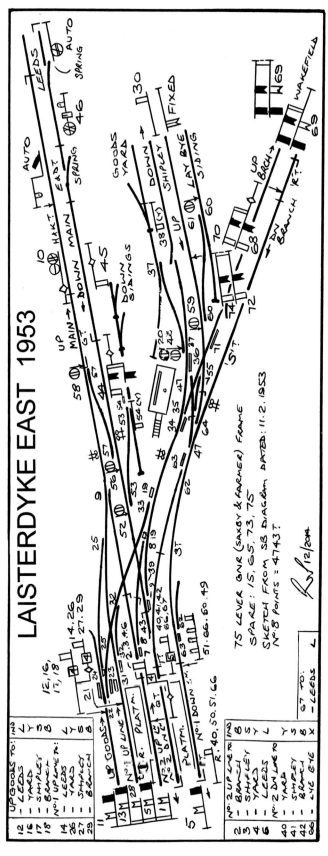

LAISTERDYKE EAST 1953

'75 LEVER GNR (SAXBY & FARMER) FRAME
SPARE: 15, 65, 73, 75
SKETCH FROM SB DIAGRAM DATED: 11.2.1953
No.8 POINTS = 47437

Nº. UP GOODS TO:	IND
12 – LEEDS	L
16 – YARD	Y
17 – SHIPLEY	S
18 – BRANCH	B

Nº.1 UP LOWER:	
14 – LEEDS	L
26 – YARD	Y
27.29 – BRANCH	B

Nº.2 UP LOWER:	IND
2 – BRANCH	B
3 – SHIPLEY	S
4 – YARD	Y
6 – LEEDS	L

Nº.2 DN LINE TO:	
40 – YARD	Y
41 – SHIPLEY	S
42 – BRANCH	B
66 – LYE B-16	X

67 TO:
– LEEDS L

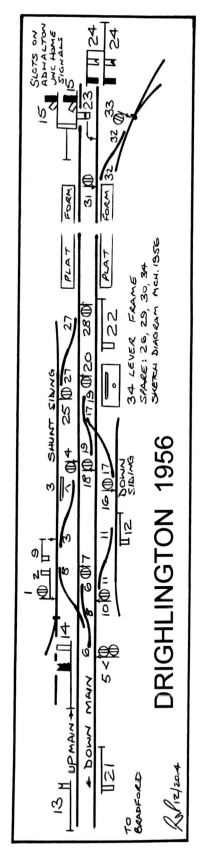

DRIGHLINGTON 1956

34 LEVER FRAME
SPARE: 26, 29, 30, 34
SKETCH DIAGRAM MCH. 1956

SLOTS ON
ADWALTON
JNC HOME
SIGNALS

TO
BRADFORD

The Telegraph Lad

Birkenshaw & Tong, looking towards Bradford in the LNER period.

A hitherto uncredited contributor to these books is David Laycock whose employment with British Railways began on 1 September 1952, the day I was born.

Over subsequent years, David supplied Peter Sunderland with Special Traffic Notices which resulted in many of the photographs appearing in these pages. In many cases, Peter was at the right location thanks to the information received from David.

Shortly after the first edition appeared in 1999, David was in touch with a new revelation. He had located the lad with a signal lever up his arse, for whom Frank Kipling called an ambulance at Laisterdyke in 1938.

The gentleman was Eric Archer, a member of David's Probus Club in Huddersfield. I was privileged to meet him and then, on his introduction, to visit Eddie Thomson. Sadly, both have since died; Eric Archer aged 87 in 2009 and Eddie Thomson aged 93 in 2007.

Eric's encounter with lever No 43 cost him eight weeks in hospital. He returned to work but in July 1939 was called up into the Royal Navy. The break in his railway career proved permanent when he came up against the LNER's arrangements for the reemployment of servicemen after the war. They were happy enough to take back the lad who had left them seven years earlier but not the naval officer into whom the lad had transformed. Eric had mistakenly believed

that he might rejoin the railway at the level which he would have reached by 1946, had his progression not been interrupted.

Eric Archer was born in 1921, the son of a Great Northern driver. He was still 15 when he joined the LNER in 1937 as a junior porter at Birkenshaw & Tong. His duties included attending the arrival of trains, calling out "Birkenshaw" and checking that the doors were all shut before signalling to the guard. Parcels, fish boxes and mail were the responsibility of the more senior porters whose main job was in the small wool warehouse. But occasionally a calf would arrive, neatly sewn into canvas with its head sticking out. Eric's job was to get on his bike and request the consignee farmer to come and collect it immediately. There were about 18 trains each way booked to stop at Birkenshaw, but none on a Sunday. The first "up" departure was the 5.09am to Wakefield Westgate via Ardsley and the last at 11.11pm via Dewsbury.

The 7.20 and 9.42am from Bradford Exchange conveyed through carriages to London, which combined with the Leeds portion at Wakefield Westgate. They stopped at Batley, Dewsbury Central and Ossett but could also be requested for London passengers at Birkenshaw & Tong, Drighlington & Adwalton and Upper Batley. A Birkenshaw mill owner would telephone the day before to arrange the stop. Eric would meet the chauffer driven car, collect the bags and escort his passenger to a position on the up platform where the first class carriage would come to a halt. A florin would change hands, representing a 15% increment on a weekly wage of 12s 6d.

The junior porter was responsible for the signal lamps. He had to walk beside the line to collect the lamps from the top of each signal. Back at the lamp room, the tinplate body was polished with pumice and rape oil. The glass was cleaned, the wick trimmed, the oil reservoir filled and the flame adjusted to give the brightest light without smoking. Then, on the return journey, he would clean the lamp case fixed to the signal, with its magnifying glass bullseye and finally the coloured aspect glasses on the semaphore.

There was little, if any, safety training. Eric had to walk through the 106 yard tunnel and could find himself at the top of a signal ladder when the arm was suddenly pulled off and engulfed in the exhaust of a passing train. But he earned a commendation from the signalling inspector after enginemen reported that Birkenshaw was showing the brightest signals in the area.

Excursions to East Coast resorts were common in summer, including evening trips which utilised some of the most ancient rolling stock available, gas lit, nongangwayed and without toilets. Eric's job was to go into the village and affix posters on the Company's bill boards.

None of which fully satisfied the ambition of the young railwayman whose attention wandered towards the signal box. The signalmen responded to his enthusiasm by teaching him aspects of their trade including Morse code and the single needle telegraph. This opened the way to Eric's first career move. In 1938, at the age of 16, he became a telegraph lad at Laisterdyke East.

Some signal boxes were too busy for the signalman to keep the register so they employed an assistant who sometimes went by the name of train recorder or booking lad. In these ex GN boxes, he was the telegraph lad because his duties included the single needle telegraph. Eric's regular mate was Bert Semper, a member of Bradford City Council who was Lord Mayor briefly in 1955 but died in office. To accommodate his civic duties, he frequently exchanged shifts with Joe Kipling or Tommy Binks giving Eric experience with all three resident signalmen and their different approaches.

When offered an up stopping train for Wakefield, Bert Samper would not accept it if it risked delaying a "Lanky" express from Leeds Central to Liverpool. But Joe Kipling would say "takk it Eric lad", meaning accept the up local, offer it forward, pull off and hope that it will be clear in time to give the express a clear run.

One Saturday morning in summer 1938, the permanent way gang were working on the track through platform 1 in Laisterdyke Station. Their tools were carried on a trolley which was too light to operate the track circuit. They were not visible from the East Box. The lookout man came to place a collar on the lever to prevent a train from being signalled through No 1 road. But as he entered the box, he became engrossed with signalman Tommy Binks on the prospects for that afternoon's football at Bradford City.

Left to run the box, Eric accepted from Laisterdyke West, a Bradford to Wakefield express on No 1 road. He immediately offered it forward to Cutlers Junction and, on acceptance, set the points and cleared the signals. As he entered the train register, he could hear the train blasting up the hill from Bradford. Suddenly, he realised what he had done. "Tommy, I've put the express up No 1". The signal levers crashed back into the frame. The lookout man gave a series of blasts on his siren to attract the ganger's attention and bellowed at him to tip the trolley onto the adjacent goods line which fortunately was vacant.

The road was reset through No 2 and the signals

4 - 6 - 0 No 5053 calls at Birkenshaw & Tong with what appears to be a works outing. The B8, built by the Great Central Railway in 1921, was shedded at Hammerton St, Bradford between 1930 and 1934. It was withdrawn for scrap in 1947.

cleared. The only thing the train suffered was having to shut off steam and lose momentum when the distant signal reverted to caution. As he passed the box, the driver gave a black look and sounded a traditional insult on the whistle.

Later in 1938, Eric felt the need for some physical exercise during a lull between trains. He was doing pressups with his back to the frame, whose levers 41, 43 and 45 were pulled off. His hands were on 41 and 45. He overbalanced backwards and became impaled on the catch of No 43. Using the omnibus circuit, the signalman contacted Frank Kipling in the ticket office with the news that the lad had a signal lever up his arse. The office had a GPO telephone with which Frank could summon an ambulance.

Eric's time in the Royal Navy lasted from 1939 until 1946, taking him from age 18 to 25. He achieved promotion, ending up in command of a motor torpedo boat. He survived many actions, including the destruction of his vessel in an attack on a convoy.

During his final year, he studied a course in modern railway operation with a view to resuming his peace time career. But when he reported to the District Superintendent in Leeds for reemployment, he was kept waiting for an hour beyond the appointed time. Then, after a brief interview, he was offered a job as a supernumerary goods porter at Bradford Adolphus Street. He was, to quote his own words, "too affronted and dismayed to make a suitable reply".

During the 1990s, Eric Archer contributed a few of his railway memories to the Yorkshire Post. The piece featuring his encounter with lever No 43 prompted a telephone call from Eddie Thomson, a retired signalling inspector who had been at Laisterdyke on that unfortunate day, 60 years earlier.

They agreed to meet over a lunch which lasted three hours, culminating in Eddie producing a photograph of the interior of Laisterdyke East with lever No 43 in focus. They exchanged reminiscences, each one reviving another in the recesses of their minds. No 8 points were a constant source of trouble. They set the route from platform 2 to either Stanningley or Cutlers Junction. They were particularly difficult because of the position of the locking bar.

Normally this would be placed between the junction signal and the facing point to prevent the point being moved whilst a train was passing over it. But here, the junction signal was so close to the point that a train stopped at it would be on the locking bar. So instead, there were locking bars on the moving blades of the point itself. This meant that when the signalman pulled the point lever, he was moving the locking bars as well. No 8 needed both muscle and frequent attention of the S & T gang.

Joe Kipling had a reputation for making good use of the S & T gang. He would call them to "come up and have a look at No 8". Then he would add "and bring the paper up too". Once they'd checked No 8 points and No 7 facing point lock, Joe would settle down with the newspaper, leaving the working of the box in the hands of the telegraph lad but still keeping a vigilant eye on proceedings. When a train was offered on the block bell, Joe would look up and say "takk it lad".

It was normal practice for the telegraph lad to gain experience on all aspects of the box, but always under the watchful eye of the signalman. This is how the next generation were trained.

No 10, the advance starter towards Leeds was reputedly the first semiautomatic colour light signal in the area, dating from the closure of Ducketts Crossing box in 1928. The down distant from Leeds was a long way from the box and round a curve. It was sometimes too much for a 9 stone, 16 year old to pull unaided. If the wires had stretched in hot weather, the arm might only dip a few degrees instead of the almost vertical somersault of the GN signal.

Occasionally, a loose coupled goods would pin down insufficient brakes for the descent from Dudley

WD class 90351 brings a short freight off the Shipley branch at Cutlers Junction. 935 "austerity" 2 – 8 – 0s were built between 1943 and 1945. 733 of them ended up with British Railways carrying numbers 90000 to 90732. All of these were scrapped between 1959 and 1967. But eventually No 90733 appeared on the Keighley & Worth Valley Railway, being one of the non BR examples having gone first to the Netherlands and then Sweden.
(Mick York/ Richard Pulleyn collection)

42116 passing Adwalton Junction on Sunday 30 October 1966 with one of the last London - Bradford portions to be routed this way. In December 1962, the signal box had been fitted with a new frame designed to last perhaps another 50 years. But within two years, Adwalton had ceased to be a junction and was gone completely in less than four.
(D J Mitchell)

Hill on greasy rails. The Laisterdyke East home signal was out of sight of the box. If it was "on", the train might fail to stop in time and the engine would peep under Dick Lane bridge, the driver no doubt mopping his brow.

The Shipley branch had already been reduced to single track and saw only sparse goods traffic. But the triangle between Laisterdyke East, Cutlers Junction and Quarry Gap was used to turn engines which came tender first from Hammerton Street shed. They then went back tender first to couple onto their trains at Bradford Exchange.

Eddie Thomson had started work in 1929 as a 15 year old member of the S&T gang based at Batley. He was in Howden Clough box on the day the photographs on page 45 were taken. The snow had begun on Friday 17 February 1933 and had fallen heavily over the weekend. Overhead lines were brought down between Howden Clough and Adwalton Junction but not, surprisingly, on the exposed section between Drighlington and Birkenshaw.

Then aged 18, Eddie was one of two telegraph linesmen based at Batley. The LNER was in the process of merging the signal and telegraph departments. There was a signal fitter and his mate at Batley and two men were sent from Stanningley. With the telegraph repair gang occupied elsewhere, this "ad hoc" gang of six worked all daylight hours over the weekend to restore normal block working. Eddie was the only one who could use climbing irons so we know who had to

do the high work. They will have secured a useful if well earned addition to their wages.

Trains were kept running under emergency regulations. At one point, the snow on the lineside was high enough to have been scored by door handles.

Three weeks later, they discovered that a block wire was trapped under a wagon wheel in Howden Clough goods yard. Because the track gave the earth return, an electric circuit was functioning between Howden Clough box and the wagon wheel.

Normal block working had been restored towards Adwalton Junction. So far as the S & T gang and the Howden Clough signalmen were aware, it was also working the other way.

The block bell was working. Each time Adwalton Junction offered a train, Howden Clough acknowledged and put his block instrument to "line clear". The Adwalton Junction signalman did not get "line clear" on his corresponding instrument but he was not unduly concerned. He knew the men were working on the telegraph and they had a lot on so he assumed they would soon get round to this remaining fault. Therefore, he would stop the train outside the box and tell the driver "block failure, pass my starter at danger, proceed at caution and be prepared to stop at any obstacle". He would then give "train entering section" on the block bell, which would be acknowledged, the two signalmen believing they had the job under control but for different reasons.

Eventually, an Adwalton Junction signalman

reported the fault only to be told that nothing was wrong. He persisted and the fault was located under the wagon wheel.

Frank Kipling had told me that his Father worked Laisterdyke East for 32 years. Eddie Thomson explained that this was very unlikely and more probable that he worked a succession of Laisterdyke boxes over that period. There so many boxes of different classes that a signalman could gain a series of promotions without having to move house. Class 5 Hall Lane Class 4 goods Quarry Gap Class 4 Broad Lane Class 3 Cutlers Junction Class 2 Laisterdyke West Class 1 Laisterdyke East Special class Hammerton Street

Class 5	Hall Lane
Class 4 goods	Quarry Gap
Class 4	Broad Lane
Class 3	Cutlers Junction
Class 2	Laisterdyke West
Class 1	Laisterdyke East
Special class	Hammerton Street

Tyersal Junction doesn't feature as, by the 1930s, it was only open for a short period around 1.45pm, which was achieved by the shifts at Cutlers Junction overlapping. One of the men walked to Tyersal to signal the 12.55pm all stations from Wakefield Westgate to Leeds Central via Batley, Dudley Hill and Pudsey, which had no return working. It was replaced from 26 September 1938 by separate trains from Wakefield to Bradford and Bradford to Leeds, connecting at Laisterdyke. The Tyersal to Broad Lane curve then had no scheduled passenger service. Tyersal Junction box became a ground frame in May 1946 and closed completely in February 1948.

The basic wage of a class 5 signalman was 50 shillings a week. Promotion to a class 4 box would give an additional 5 shillings, class 3 another 5 shillings and so on to class 1 at 70 shillings a week. Hammerton Street was worth 75 shillings. A class 4 goods box was half way from class 5 to 4.

A class 2 signalman was on the same basic wage as a passenger guard at 65 shillings a week. Eddie Thomson thought that the former carried the greater responsibility and required more physical effort. It was the box which was classified, not the man. The class depended on the number of lever movements and other activities such as telegraph messages. It was determined by a marks committee from evidence gathered by a relief signalman, always from a different area, who sat in the box to record the number of transactions.

On the day of the visit, the box could be particularly busy. Tricks included the shunting engine taking a wagon out of the yard and then returning for a second one which had conveniently been forgotten. In some boxes, an extra half mark was given each time the signalman had to press a foot stud to release a lever which was interlocked to prevent a false move. Before the lever could be pulled, other relevant points and

Track renewal at Laisterdyke East on Sunday 3 July 1921. The signals from both Quarry Gap and Cutlers Junction offer a choice of route through Laisterdyke Station. They carry distant signals for Laisterdyke West and are duplicated for sighting at high and low level. East box lasted from 1892 until 1979, the last nine years only as a 7 lever ground frame.

Just north of Howden Clough, the GN crossed the LNW "Leeds New Line". "Black Five" No 45208 is in charge of the Bradford portion of a train from London Kings Cross in July 1962. *(Peter Sunderland)*

signals had all to be in the correct position. The lock, beneath the frame down in the locking room, was lifted by an electric current. But if this was switched on permanently, the batteries would quickly be drained. So the foot stud activated the current just long enough for the move to be made.

When the night shift was abolished at Batley, one of the signalmen did a bit of arithmetic and asked for a regrading from class 4 to 3. Without the quieter nocturnal hours, the number of movements per shift had risen.

Some signalmen appeared content to stay in one place, perhaps working a class 5 box for most of their lives. Others would move to the other end of the system to gain a promotion. The Company would pay removal expenses for a promotion but not for a sideways move.

Eligibility for promotion was by seniority – that is length of service not age. If there was more than one suitable applicant for a post, the one with greatest seniority would get it. Occasionally, a signalman could leapfrog the system. Vacancy lists came round with the weekly traffic notice. One man might decide there was no point in applying because "so and so" was ahead on seniority. But if "so and so" himself didn't apply, the job could go to somebody further back in seniority who had applied just on the off chance.

During a number of winters, Tom Chapman left Howden Clough (class 5) to work Thorpe Lane, a class 4 goods box between Tingley and Ardsley West. By doing this, Tom gained half a crown extra on his basic wage, a 5% increment, plus the possibility of Sunday and night enhancements which were not available at Howden Clough. Thorpe Lane functioned only on the up goods line. It saw increased activity in winter, mainly shunting empty wagons in and out of the sidings. There was permissive block from Tingley to Thorpe Lane. A train could be signalled on the up goods without confirmation that the previous one had cleared the section.

During the Second World War, an S&T linesman was in a reserved occupation, exempt from military service. Eddie Thompson was invited to apply for a promotion for which he was eligible on seniority. He said he wasn't interested because he wasn't prepared to move house. The Rule Book required staff to reside where the Company directed. Eddie was told that the rule had been overtaken by the exigencies of war. If he could get to work by bicycle, goods train or any means at his disposal, then he could have the job and stay living where he was.

Eddie remained on the Railway all his working life, retiring as a signal inspector in the late 1970s. BR availed of his long experience by keeping him on the declining number of manual installations.

Single needle telegraph

The telegraph was similar in appearance to a block

instrument, with a dial upon which a needle moved to the left for a dot and the right for a dash. At the same time, it made a sharper sound for the dot and a flatter tone for the dash. The "reader" could rely on watching the needle, hearing the tones or both according to preference and experience. Messages were sent in Morse code by turning a handle at the base of the machine to the left and right.

Signal boxes were linked by omnibus circuits. There was one from Wakefield Westgate to Laisterdyke and another from Leeds Central to Ossett so Batley and Dewsbury had instruments on both.

A signalman would ignore the telegraph until he heard his own call sign e.g. BT for Batley. This he would acknowledge by repeating. Then the caller would identify himself e.g. OT for Ossett West. The recipient would then give a T or G according to his own degree of confidence in receiving Morse. T meant break it up with spaces between words. G meant send without any breaks.

The Great Northern may originally have been a leader in the field of communication between signal boxes. But in the 20th Century, they were still telegraphing when some other companies were speaking on telephones. At Batley, the GN signalman was trained on the telegraph but his close neighbour in the LNW box wasn't.

The Trolley Block

In the early 1930s, the LNER reorganised the permanent way men from small local gangs into larger mobile teams who travelled with their equipment on a motorised trolley.

The trolley was "parked" on a short siding at right angles to the running rails. It could be manoeuvred onto the main line with the help of a small turntable carried on the vehicle. Before this could happen, the trolley driver had to call the signal box on his handset, which he plugged in to an adjacent telegraph pole. The signalman heard him over a loud speaker and then went to the trolley telephone by the lever frame. The movement had to be agreed with the signalmen at both ends of the block section. The driver was given a release enabling him to withdraw the trolley token from its cupboard in a p w hut or attached to a telegraph pole. The principle was rather like that where a driver takes a single line token from a remote instrument. The effect was to lock normal block working in the affected section.

When the gang had finished work, or knew that it had to be interrupted for a train to pass, the trolley would be returned to its siding. The driver would telephone the signalman to report that the main line was clear. He would then give a release by means of a.c. generated on his handset. This release allowed normal block working to resume. It had to be by a.c. because there was a lot of equipment in the signal box powered by d.c. which is capable of straying. There had to be no risk of block working being released by accident whilst a trolley was on the line. On some routes, it was difficult to find a gap in the train service, long enough for the trolley to do much. On other lines, this was no problem but Eddie Thomson doubted whether the trolley block was ever worth the investment. It did however have an unintended by product.

The trolley driver could speak to the signalmen at both ends of the section. This also meant that they could speak to each other. It was very tempting for them to use the trolley telephone instead of the telegraph, not just for official traffic but also for more general chit chat. Some signalmen found their skill on the telegraph getting rusty but the system remained in place until most of the ex GN boxes closed in the 1960s.

Appendices

Leeds, Bradford & Halifax Junction

Opened

01.08.1854	Leeds Central - Bowling Jn
01.08.1854	Laisterdyke - Adolphus St
07.01.1867	Hammerton St - Bradford Ex

Closed to passengers

06.01.1867	Hammerton St - Adolphus St
31.12.1961	Laisterdyke - Bowling Jn

Closed to all traffic

29.04.1967	Leeds Central - Holbeck
28.04.1972	Hammerton St - Adolphus St
30.09.1985	Laisterdyke - Bowling Jn

Miles	Stations	Opened	Closed
0	Leeds Central	18.09.1848	29.04.1967
½	Holbeck	02.07.1855	05.07.1958
2	Armley Moor	01.08.1854	02.07.1966
4	Bramley	01.08.1854	02.07.1966
5½	Stanningley	01.08.1854	30.12.1967
6	New Pudsey	06.03.1967	
7½	Laisterdyke	01.08.1854	02.07.1966
–	Bowling	01.08.1854	31.01.1895
–	Bradford Adolphus St	01.08.1854	06.01.1867
9	St Dunstan`s	21.11.1878	13.09.1952
9½	Bradford Exchange	09.05.1850	

Bramley reopened on 12.09.1983

Methley Joint

Opened

Jan 1865	Goods
01.05.1869	Passengers

Closed

31.10.1964	Passengers
03.04.1965	West of Newmarket Colliery
25.03.1967	Methley South - Joint Jn
21.02.1981	East of Newmarket Colliery

0	Ardsley	05.10.1857	31.10.1964
3¾	Stanley	01.05.1869	31.10.1964
6¼	Methley South	01.05.1869	05.03.1960
7¾	Castleford Central	01.07.1840	

Doncaster, Wakefield and Leeds

Opened
05.10.1857	Ings Road Jn (W'field) - Wortley S and W	
01.02.1866	Doncaster - Ings Road Jn	

Closed
30.09.1984	Wortley S Jn - Wortley W Jn	

Stations reopened
01.03.1982	Fitzwilliam
30.11.1987	Sandal & Agbrigg
12.07.1988	Outwood
11.10.1993	Adwick

0	Doncaster	07.09.1848	
1¾	Bentley	17.05.1993	
4	Carcroft & Adwick le Street	01.02.1866	04.11.1967
6	Hampole	01.01.1885	05.01.1952
8½	South Elmsall	01.02.1866	
11¾	Hemsworth	01.02.1866	04.11.1967
13¼	Fitzwilliam	01.06.1937	04.11.1967
14¼	Nostell	01.02.1866	27.10.1951
16	Hare Park & Crofton	01.11.1886	02.02.1952
18	Sandal	01.02.1866	02.11.1957
19¾	Wakefield Westgate	05.10.1857	
22¼	Lofthouse & Outwood	05.10.1857	11.06.1960
24¼	Ardsley	05.10.1857	31.10.1964
27¼	Beeston	01.02.1860	01.03.1953
29¼	Holbeck	02.07.1855	05.07.1958
29¾	Leeds Central	18.09.1848	29.04.1967

Ardsley to Laisterdyke

Opened
20.08.1856	Gildersome - Laisterdyke
10.10.1857	Ardsley - Gildersome

Closed
03.07.1966	Passengers
30.10.1966	Gildersome - Birkenshaw
13.03.1968	Morley Top - Gildersome
13.03.1968	Birkenshaw - Dudley Hill
1969	Ardsley - Morley Top
1981	Dudley Hill - Laisterdyke

0	Ardsley	05.10.1857	31.10.1964
1½	Tingley	01.05.1859	30.01.1954
2½	Morley Top	10.10.1857	31.12.1960
4¼	Gildersome	20.08.1856	11.06.1955
5½	Drighlington & Adwalton	20.08.1856	30.12.1961
6½	Birkenshaw & Tong	20.08.1856	03.10.1953
8¼	Dudley Hill	20.08.1856	05.04.1952
10¼	Laisterdyke	01.08.1854	02.07.1966

Wakefield to Drighlington

Opened
Jan 1862	Wrenthorpe - Roundwood Coll (goods)
07.04.1862	Wakefield Westgate - Flushdyke
19.08.1863	Upper Batley - Drighlington & Adwalton
02.04.1864	Flushdyke - Ossett
01.11.1864	Batley - Upper Batley
15.12.1864	Ossett - Batley
09.09.1874	Ossett - Dewsbury (temp station)
15.03.1880	Dewsbury Junction - Batley Carr
12.04.1880	Batley Carr - Batley

Closed to Passengers
30.06.1909	Ossett - Batley
05.09.1964	Wakefield Westgate - Adwalton Junction

Closed to all traffic
24.03.1956	Runtlings Junction - Shaw Cross Colliery
13.02.1965	Roundwood Colliery - Adwalton Junction
29.10.1865	Wrenthorpe - Roundwood Colliery
29.04.1972	Shaw Cross - Batley

0	Wakefield Westgate	05.10.1857	
1¾	Alverthorpe	01.10.1872	03.04.1954
3	Flushdyke	07.04.1862	03.05.1941
3¾	Ossett	02.04.1864	05.09.1964
–	Chickenley Heath	02.07.1877	30.06.1909
5¼	Earlsheaton	01.01.1875	06.06.1953
–	Dewsbury (temp station)	09.09.1874	14.03.1880
6¼	Dewsbury Central	15.03.1880	05.09.1964
6¾	Batley Carr	15.03.1880	04.03.1950
7¾	Batley	18.09.1848	
8½	Upper Batley	19.08.1863	02.02.1952
9¼	Howden Clough	01.11.1866	29.11.1952
10¾	Drighlington & Adwalton	20.08.1856	30.12.1961

Batley to Beeston

Opened
Late 1887	Batley - Soothlll Colliery (goods)
01.08.1890	Batley - Tingley - Beeston

Closed
27.10.1951	Passengers
04.07.1953	Batley - Woodkirk
04.07.1953	Tingley - Beeston
28.06.1964	Woodkirk - Tingley

0	Batley	18.09.1848	
1¾	Woodkirk	01.08.1890	23.09.1939
3	Tingley	01.05.1859	30.01.1954
5¾	Beeston	01.02.1860	01.03.1953

Pudsey Loop

Opened
1877	Stanningley - Pudsey Greenside (goods)
01.04.1878	Stanningley - Pudsey Greenside (passr)
01.11.1893	Bramley - Laisterdyke
01.12.1893	Pudsey Greenside - Low Moor

Closed to Passengers
21.08.1911	Dudley Hill - Low Moor
24.09.1938	Pudsey Greenside - Dudley Hill
13.06.1964	Bramley - Laisterdyke

Closed to all traffic
09.05.1933	Dudley Hill - Low Moor
1948	Tyersal Jn - Broad Lane Jn
03.07.1964	Bramley - Laisterdyke

0	Bramley	01.08.1854	02.07.1966
1¼	Pudsey Lowtown	01.07.1878	13.06.1964
1¾	Pudsey Greenside	01.04.1878	13.06.1964
3¾	Laisterdyke	01.08.1854	02.07.1966
4½	Dudley Hill	20.08.1856	05.04.1952
6¼	Low Moor	09.07.1848	12.06.1965